THE EVE OF THE REVOLUTION

TEXTBOOK EDITION

∴

THE YALE CHRONICLES
OF AMERICA SERIES
ALLEN JOHNSON
EDITOR

GERHARD R. LOMER
CHARLES W. JEFFERYS
ASSISTANT EDITORS

THE EVE OF
THE REVOLUTION

A CHRONICLE OF THE
BREACH WITH ENGLAND
BY CARL BECKER

TORONTO: GLASGOW, BROOK & CO.
NEW YORK: UNITED STATES PUBLISHERS
ASSOCIATION, INC.

PREFACE

In this brief sketch I have chiefly endeavored to convey to the reader, not a record of what men did, but a sense of how they thought and felt about what they did. To give the quality and texture of the state of mind and feeling of an individual or class, to create for the reader the illusion (not *delusion*, O able Critic!) of the intellectual atmosphere of past times, I have as a matter of course introduced many quotations; but I have also ventured to resort frequently to the literary device (this, I know, gives the whole thing away) of telling the story by means of a rather free paraphrase of what some imagined spectator or participant might have thought or said about the matter in hand. If the critic says that the product of such methods is not history, I am willing to call it by any name that is better; the point of greatest relevance being the truth and effectiveness of the

illusion aimed at—the extent to which it reproduces the quality of the thought and feeling of those days, the extent to which it enables the reader to enter into such states of mind and feeling. The truth of such history (or whatever the critic wishes to call it) cannot of course be determined by a mere verification of references.

To one of my colleagues, who has read the entire manuscript, I am under obligations for many suggestions and corrections in matters of detail; and I would gladly mention his name if it could be supposed that an historian of established reputation would wish to be associated, even in any slight way, with an enterprise of questionable orthodoxy.

CARL BECKER.

ITHACA, NEW YORK,
January 6, 1918.

CONTENTS

CONTENTS

THE EVE OF THE REVOLUTION

. .

CHAPTER I

A PATRIOT OF 1763

His Majesty's reign . . . I predict will be happy and truly glorious. — *Benjamin Franklin.*

THE 29th of January, 1757, was a notable day in the life of Ben Franklin of Philadelphia, well known in the metropolis of America as printer and politician, and famous abroad as a scientist and Friend of the Human Race. It was on that day that the Assembly of Pennsylvania commissioned him as its agent to repair to London in support of its petition against the Proprietors of the Province, who were charged with having "obstinately persisted in manacling their deputies [the Governors of Pennsylvania] with instructions inconsistent not only with the privileges of the people, but with the service of the Crown." We

1

may, therefore, if we choose, imagine the philosopher on that day, being then in his fifty-first year, walking through the streets of this metropolis of America (a town of something less than twenty thousand inhabitants) to his modest home, and there informing his "Dear Debby" that her husband, now apparently become a great man in a small world, was ordered immediately "home to England."

In those leisurely days, going home to England was no slight undertaking; and immediately, when there was any question of a great journey, meant as soon as the gods might bring it to pass. "I had agreed with Captain Morris, of the Pacquet at New York, for my passage," he writes in the *Autobiography*, "and my stores were put on board, when Lord Loudoun arrived at Philadelphia, expressly, as he told me, to endeavor an accommodation between the Governor and the Assembly, that his Majesty's service might not be obstructed by their dissentions." Franklin was the very man to effect an accommodation, when he set his mind to it, as he did on this occasion; but "in the mean time," he relates, "the Pacquet had sailed with my sea stores, which was some loss to me, and my only recompence was his Lordship's thanks for my service, all the credit for obtaining the accommodation falling to his share."

It was now war time, and the packets were at the disposal of Lord Loudoun, commander of the forces in America. The General was good enough to inform his accommodating friend that of the two packets then at New York, one was given out to sail on Saturday, the 12th of April — "but," the great man added very confidentially, "I may let you know, *entre nous*, that if you are there by Monday morning, you will be in time, but do not delay longer." As early as the 4th of April, accordingly, the provincial printer and Friend of the Human Race, accompanied by many neighbors "to see him out of the province," left Philadelphia. He arrived at Trenton "well before night," and expected, in case "the roads were no worse," to reach Woodbridge by the night following. In crossing over to New York on the Monday, some accident at the ferry delayed him, so that he did not reach the city till nearly noon, and he feared that he might miss the packet after all — Lord Loudoun had so precisely mentioned Monday morning. Happily, no such thing! The packet was still there. It did not sail that day, or the next either; and as late as the 29th of April

Franklin was still hanging about waiting to be off. For it was war time and the packets waited the orders of General Loudoun, who, ready in promises but slow in execution, was said to be "like St. George on the signs, always on horseback but never rides on."

Franklin himself was a deliberate man, and at the last moment he decided, for some reason or other, not to take the first packet. Behold him, therefore, waiting for the second through the month of May and the greater part of June! "This tedious state of uncertainty and long waiting," during which the agent of the Province of Pennsylvania, running back and forth from New York to Woodbridge, spent his time more uselessly than ever he remembered, was duly credited to the perversity of the British General. But at last they were off, and on the 26th of July, three and a half months after leaving Philadelphia, Franklin arrived in London to take up the work of his mission; and there he remained, always expecting to return shortly, but always delayed, for something more than five years.

These were glorious days in the history of Old England, the most heroic since the reign of Good Queen Bess. When the provincial printer arrived

in London, the King and the politicians had already
been forced, through multiplied reverses in every
part of the world, to confer power upon William
Pitt, a disagreeable man indeed, but still a great
genius and War Lord, who soon turned defeat
into victory. It was the privilege of Franklin,
here in the capital of the Empire, to share the
exaltation engendered by those successive con-
quests that gave India and America to the little
island kingdom, and made Englishmen, in Horace
Walpole's phrase, "heirs apparent of the Romans."
No Briton rejoiced more sincerely than this provincial American in the extension of the Empire.
He labored with good will and good humor, and
doubtless with good effect, to remove popular
prejudice against his countrymen; and he wrote
a masterly pamphlet to prove the wisdom of retaining Canada rather than Guadaloupe at the
close of the war, confidently assuring his readers
that the colonies would never, even when once
the French danger was removed, "unite against
their own nation, which protects and encourages
them, with which they have so many connections
and ties of blood, interest, and affection, and which
'tis well known they all love much more than
they love one another."

Franklin, at least, loved Old England, and it might well be maintained that these were the happiest years of his life. He was mentally so cosmopolitan, so much at ease in the world, that here in London he readily found himself at home indeed. The business of his particular mission, strictly attended to, occupied no great part of his time. He devoted long days to his beloved scientific experiments, and carried on a voluminous correspondence with David Hume and Lord Kames, and with many other men of note in England, France, and Italy. He made journeys, to Holland, to Cambridge, to ancestral places and the homes of surviving relatives; but mostly, one may imagine, he gave himself to a steady flow of that "agreeable and instructive conversation" of which he was so much the master and the devotee. He was more famous than he knew, and the reception that everywhere awaited him was flattering, and as agreeable to his unwarped and emancipated mind as it was flattering. "The regard and friendship I meet with," he confesses, "and the conversation of ingenious men, give me no small pleasure"; and at Cambridge, "my vanity was not a little gratified by the particular regard shown me by the Chancellor and Vice-

Chancellor of the University, and the Heads of the Colleges." As the years passed, the sense of being at ease among friends grew stronger; the serene and placid letters to "Dear Debby" became rather less frequent; the desire to return to America was much attenuated.

How delightful, indeed, was this Old England! "Of all the enviable things England has," he writes, "I envy it most its people. . . . Why should this little island enjoy in almost every neighborhood more sensible, virtuous, and elegant minds, than we can collect in ranging one hundred leagues of our vast forests?" What a proper place for a philosopher to spin out the remnant of his days! The idea had occurred to him; he was persistently urged by his friend William Strahan to carry it into effect; and his other friend, David Hume, made him a pretty compliment on the same theme: "America has sent us many good things, gold, silver, sugar, tobacco; but you are the first philosopher for whom we are beholden to her. It is our own fault that we have not kept him; whence it appears that we do not agree with Solomon, that wisdom is above gold; for we take good care never to send back an ounce of the latter, which we once lay our fingers upon." The philosopher was willing enough to remain; and of the two objections which he mentioned to Strahan, the rooted aversion of his wife to embarking on the ocean and his love for Philadelphia, the latter for the moment clearly gave him less difficulty than the former. "I cannot leave this happy island and my friends in it without extreme regret," he writes at the moment of departure. "I am going from the old world to the new; and I fancy I feel like those who are leaving this world for the next; grief at the parting; fear of the passage; hope for the future."

When, on the 1st of November, 1762, Franklin quietly slipped into Philadelphia, he found that the new world had not forgotten him. For many days his house was filled from morning till night with a succession of friends, old and new, come to congratulate him on his return; excellent people all, no doubt, and yet presenting, one may suppose, a rather sharp contrast to the "virtuous and elegant minds" from whom he had recently parted in England. The letters he wrote, immediately following his return to America, to his friends William Strahan and Mary Stevenson lack something of the cheerful and contented good humor which is Franklin's most characteristic tone. His

thoughts, like those of a homesick man, are ever
dwelling on his English friends, and he still nour-
ishes the fond hope of returning, bag and baggage,
to England for good and all. The very letter
which he begins by relating the cordiality of his
reception in Philadelphia he closes by assuring
Strahan that "in two years at fartherest I hope
to settle all my affairs in such manner as that
I may then conveniently remove to England —
provided," he adds as an afterthought, "we can
persuade the good woman to cross the sea. That
will be the great difficulty."

It is not known whether it was this difficulty
that prevented the eminent doctor, revered in two
continents for his wisdom, from changing the place
of his residence. Dear Debby, as docile as a child
in most respects, very likely had her settled
prejudices, of which the desire to remain on dry
land may have been one, and one of the most obstinate. Or it may be that Franklin found himself too much occupied, too much involved in
affairs after his long absence, to make even a
beginning in his cherished plan; or else, as the
months passed and he settled once more to the
familiar, humdrum life of the American metropolis,
sober second thought may have revealed to him

what was doubtless a higher wisdom. "Business, public and private, devours my time," he writes in March, 1764. "I must return to England for repose. With such thoughts I flatter myself, and need some kind friend to put me often in mind *that old trees cannot safely be transplanted.*" Perhaps, after all, Dear Debby was this kind friend; in which case Americans must all, to this day, be much indebted to the good woman.

At least it was no apprehension of difficulties arising between England and the colonies that induced Franklin to remain in America. The Peace of Paris he regarded as "the most advantageous" of any recorded in British annals, very fitting to mark the close of a successful war, and well suited to usher in the long period of prosperous felicity which should properly distinguish the reign of a virtuous prince. Never before, in Franklin's opinion, were the relations between Britain and her colonies more happy; and there could be, he thought, no good reason to fear that the excellent young King would be distressed, or his prerogative diminished, by factitious parliamentary opposition.

You now fear for our virtuous young King, that the faction forming will overpower him and render his reign uncomfortable [he writes to Strahan]. On the contrary, I am of opinion that his virtue and the consciousness of his sincere intentions to make his people happy will give him firmness and steadiness in his measures and in the support of the honest friends he has chosen to serve him; and when that firmness is fully perceived, faction will dissolve and be dissipated like a morning fog before the rising sun, leaving the rest of the day clear with a sky serene and cloudless. Such after a few of the first years will be the future course of his Majesty's reign, which I predict will be happy and truly glorious. A new war I cannot yet see reason to apprehend. The peace will I think long continue, and your nation be as happy as they deserve to be.

CHAPTER II

THE BURDEN OF EMPIRE

Nothing of note in Parliament, except one slight day on the American taxes. — Horace Walpole.

THERE were plenty of men in England, any time before 1763, who found that an excellent arrangement which permitted them to hold office in the colonies while continuing to reside in London. They were thereby enabled to make debts, and sometimes even to pay them, without troubling much about their duties; and one may easily think of them, over their claret, as Mr. Trevelyan says, lamenting the cruelty of a secretary of state who hinted that, for form's sake at least, they had best show themselves once in a while in America. They might have replied with Junius: "It was not Virginia that wanted a governor, but a court favorite that wanted a salary " Certainly Virginia could do with a minimum of royal officials; but most court favorites wanted salaries, for without salaries unendowed gentlemen could not conveniently live in London.

One of these gentlemen, in the year 1763, was Mr. Grosvenor Bedford. He was not, to be sure, a court favorite, but a man, now well along in years, who had long ago been appointed to be Collector of the Customs at the port of Philadelphia. The appointment had been made by the great minister, Robert Walpole, for whom Mr. Bedford had unquestionably done some service or other, and of whose son, Horace Walpole, the letter-writer, he had continued from that day to be a kind of dependent or protégé, being precisely the sort of unobtrusive factotum which that fastidious eccentric needed to manage his mundane affairs. But now, after this long time, when the King's business was placed in the hands of George Grenville, who entertained the odd notion that a Collector of the Customs should reside at the port of entry where the customs were collected rather than in London where he drew his salary, it was being noised about, and was presently reported at Strawberry Hill, that Mr. Bedford, along with many other estimable gentlemen, was forthwith to be turned out of his office.

To Horace Walpole it was a point of more than

academic importance to know whether gentlemen were to be unceremoniously turned out of their offices. As far back as 1738, while still a lad, he had himself been appointed to be Usher of the Exchequer; and as soon as he came of age, he says, "I took possession of two other little patent places in the Exchequer, called Comptroller of the Pipe, and Clerk of the Estreats" — all these places having been procured for him through the generosity of his father. The duties of these offices, one may suppose, were not arduous, for it seems that they were competently administered by Mr. Grosvenor Bedford, in addition to his duties as Collector of the Customs at the port of Philadelphia; so well administered, indeed, that Horace Walpole's income from them, which in 1740 was perhaps not more than £1500 a year, nearly doubled in the course of a generation. And this income, together with another thousand which he had annually from the Collector's place in the Custom House, added to the interest of £20,000 which he had inherited, enabled him to live very well, with immense leisure for writing odd books, and letters full of extremely interesting comment on the levity and low aims of his contemporaries.

And so Horace Walpole, good patron that he

was and competent letter-writer, very naturally, hearing that Mr. Bedford was to lose an office to which in the course of years he had become much accustomed, sat down and wrote a letter to Mr. George Grenville in behalf of his friend and servant. "Though I am sensible I have no pretensions for asking you a favour, . . . yet I flatter myself I shall not be thought quite impertinent in interceding for a person, who I can answer has neither been to blame nor any way deserved punishment, and therefore I think you, Sir, will be ready to save him from prejudice. The person I mean is my deputy, Mr. Grosvenor Bedford, who, above five and twenty years ago, was appointed Collector of the Customs in Philadelphia by my father. I hear he is threatened to be turned out. If the least fault can be laid to his charge, I do not desire to have him protected. If there cannot, I am too well persuaded, Sir, of your justice not to be sure you will be pleased to protect him."

George Grenville, a dry, precise man of great knowledge and industry, almost always right in little matters and very patient of the misapprehensions of less exact people, wrote in reply a letter which many would think entirely adequate to the matter in hand:

I have never heard [he began] of any complaint against Mr. Grosvenor Bedford, or of any desire to turn him out; but by the office which you tell me he holds in North America, I believe I know the state of the case, which I will inform you of, that you may be enabled to judge of it yourself. Heavy complaints were last year made in Parliament of the state of our revenues in North America which amount to between £1,000 and £2,000 a year, the collecting of which costs upon the establishment of the Customs in Great Britain between £7,000 and £8,000 a year.   This, it was urged, arose from the making all these offices sinecures in England.   When I came to the Treasury[1] I directed the Commissioners of the Customs to be written to, that they might inform us how the revenue might be improved, and to what causes they attributed the present diminished state of it. . . .   The principal cause which they assigned was the absence of the officers who lived in England by leave of the Treasury, which they proposed should be recalled. This we complied with, and ordered them all to their duty, and the Commissioners of the Customs to present others in the room of such as should not obey.   I take it for granted that this is Mr. Bedford's case. If it is, it will be attended with difficulty to make an exception, as they are every one of them applying to be excepted out of the orders. . . .   If it is not so, or if Mr. Bedford can suggest to me any proper means of obviating it without overturning the whole regulation, he will do me a sensible pleasure.

[1] On the resignation of Lord Bute in April, 1763, Grenville formed a ministry, himself taking the two offices of First Lord of the Treasury and Chancellor of the Exchequer.

There is no evidence to show that Mr. Bedford was able to do Mr. Grenville this "sensible pleasure." The incident, apparently closed, was one of many indications that a new policy for dealing with America was about to be inaugurated; and although Grenville had been made minister for reasons that were remote enough from any question of efficiency in government, no better man could have been chosen for applying to colonial administration the principles of good business management. His connection with the Treasury, as well as the natural bent of his mind, had made him "confessedly the ablest man of business in the House of Commons." The Governors of the Bank of England, very efficient men certainly, held it a great point in the minister's favor that they "could never do business with any man with the same ease they had done it with him." Undoubtedly the first axiom of business is that one's accounts should be kept straight, one's books nicely balanced; the second, that one's assets should exceed one's liabilities. Mr. Grenville, accordingly, "had studied the revenues with professional assiduity, and something of professional ideas seemed to mingle in all his regulations concerning them." He "felt the

weight of debt, amounting at this time to one
hundred and fifty-eight millions, which oppressed
his country, and he looked to the amelioration of
the revenue as the only mode of relieving it."

It is true there were some untouched sources of
revenue still available in England. As sinecures
went in that day, Mr. Grosvenor Bedford's was not
of the best; and on any consideration of the matter
from the point of view of revenue only, Grenville
might well have turned his attention to a different
class of officials; for example, to the Master of the
Rolls in Ireland, Mr. Rigby, who was also Paymaster of the Forces, and to whose credit there
stood at the Bank of England, as Mr. Trevelyan
assures us, a million pounds of the public money,
the interest of which was paid to him "or to his
creditors." This was a much better thing than
Grosvenor Bedford had with his paltry collector·
ship at Philadelphia; and the interest on a million
pounds, more or less, had it been diverted from
Mr. Rigby's pocket to the public treasury, would
perhaps have equaled the entire increase in the
revenue to be expected from even the most efficient administration of the customs in all the
ports of America. In addition, it should perhaps
be said that Mr. Rigby, although excelled by none,

was by no means the only man in high place with a good degree of talent for exploiting the common chest.

The reform of such practices, very likely, was work for a statesman rather than for a man of business. A good man of business, called upon to manage the King's affairs, was likely to find many obstacles in the way of depriving the Paymaster of the Forces of his customary sources of income, and Mr. Grenville, at least, never attempted anything so hazardous. Scurrilous pamphleteers, in fact, had made it a charge against the minister that he had increased rather than diminished the evil of sinecures—"It had been written in pamphlets that £400,000 a year was dealt out in pensions"; from which charge the able Chancellor, on the occasion of opening his first budget in the House of Commons, the 9th of March, 1764, defended himself by denying that the sums were "so great as alleged." It was scarcely an adequate defense; but the truth is that Grenville was sure to be less distressed by a bad custom, no law forbidding, than by a law, good or bad, not strictly enforced, particularly if the law was intended to bring in a revenue.

Instinctively, therefore, the minister turned to

America, where it was a notorious fact that there were revenue laws that had not been enforced these many years.   Mr. Grenville, we may suppose, since it was charged against him in a famous epigram, read the American dispatches with considerable care, so that it is quite possible he may have chanced to see and to shake his head over the sworn statement of Mr. Sampson Toovey, a statement which throws much light upon colonial liberties and the practices of English officials in those days:

I, Sampson Toovey [so the statement runs], Clerk to James Cockle, Esq., Collector of His Majesty's Customs for the Port of Salem, do declare on oath, that ever since I have been in the office, it hath been customary for said Cockle to receive of the masters of vessels entering from Lisbon, casks of wine, boxes of fruit, etc., which was a gratuity for suffering their vessels to be entered with salt or ballast only, and passing over unnoticed such cargoes of wine, fruit, etc., which are prohibited to be imported into His Majesty's plantations.   Part of which wine, fruit, etc., the said James Cockle used to share with Governor Bernard. And I further declare that I used to be the negotiator of this business, and receive the wine, fruit, etc., and dispose of them agreeable to Mr. Cockle's orders. Witness my hand.   Sampson Toovey.

The curious historian would like much to know, in case Mr. Grenville did see the declaration of Samp-

son Toovey, whether he saw also a letter in which
Governor Bernard gave it as his opinion that if
the colonial governments were to be refashioned it
should be on a new plan, since "there is no system
in North America fit to be made a module of."

Secretary Grenville, whether or not he ever saw
this letter from Governor Bernard, was familiar
with the ideas which inspired it. Most crown
officials in America, and the governors above
all, finding themselves little more than executive
agents of the colonial assemblies, had long clam-
ored for the remodeling of colonial governments:
the charters, they said, should be recalled; the
functions of the assemblies should be limited
and more precisely defined; judges should be appointed at the pleasure of the King; and judges
and governors alike should be paid out of a permanent civil list in England drawn from revenue raised in America. In urging these changes,
crown officials in America were powerfully supported by men of influence in England; by Halifax since the day, some fifteen years before, when
he was appointed to the office of Colonial Secretary; by the brilliant Charles Townshend who,
in the year 1763, as first Lord of the Treasury
in Bute's ministry, had formulated a bill which

would have been highly pleasing to Governor Bernard had it been passed into law. And now similar schemes were being urged upon Grenville by his own colleagues, notably by the Earl of Halifax, who is said to have become, in a formal interview with the first minister, extremely heated and eager in the matter.

But all to no purpose. Mr. Grenville was well content with the form of the colonial governments, being probably of Pope's opinion that "the system that is best administered is best." In Grenville's opinion, the Massachusetts government was good enough, and all the trouble arose from the inattention of royal officials to their manifest duties and from the pleasant custom of depositing at Governor Bernard's back door sundry pipes of wine with the compliments of Mr. Cockle. Most men in England agreed that such pleasant customs had been tolerated long enough. To their suppression the first minister accordingly gave his best attention; and while Mr. Rigby continued to enjoy great perquisites in England, many obscure customs officials, such as Grosvenor Bedford, were ordered to their posts to prevent small peculations in America. To assist them, or their successors, in this business, ships of war were stationed conveniently for the

intercepting of smugglers, general writs were au
thorized to facilitate the search for goods ille-
gally entered, and the governors, His Excellency
Governor Bernard among the number, were newly
instructed to give their best efforts to the enforcement of the trade acts.

All this was but an incident, to be sure, in the
minister's general scheme for "ameliorating the
revenue." It was not until the 9th of March,
1764, that Grenville, "not disguising how much
he was hurt by abuse," opened his first budget,
"fully, for brevity was not his failing," and still
with great "art and ability." Although ministers
were to be congratulated, he thought, "on the
revenue being managed with more frugality than
in the late reign," the House scarcely need be told
that the war had greatly increased the debt, an
increase not to be placed at a lower figure than
some seventy odd millions; and so, on account of
this great increase in the debt, and in spite of
gratifying advances in the customs duties and
the salutary cutting off of the German subsidies,
taxes were now, the House would easily understand, necessarily much higher than formerly —
"our taxes," he said, "exceeded by three millions
what they were in 1754." Much money, doubtless.

could still be raised on the land tax, if the House
was at all disposed to put on another half shilling in the pound. Ministers could take it quite
for granted, however, that country squires, sitting
on the benches, would not be disposed to increase
the land tax, but would much prefer some skillful
manipulation of the colonial customs, provided
only there was some one who understood that art
well enough to explain to the House where such
duties were meant to fall and how much they might
reasonably be expected to bring in. And there,
in fact, was Mr. Grenville explaining it all with
"art and ability," for which task, indeed, there
could be none superior to his Majesty's Chancellor
of the Exchequer, who had so long "studied the
revenue with professional assiduity."

The items of the budget, rather dull reading now
and none too illuminating, fell pleasantly upon
the ears of country squires sitting there on the
benches; and the particular taxes no doubt seemed
reasonably clear to them, even if they had no
perfect understanding of the laws of incidence,
inasmuch as sundry of the new duties apparently
fell upon the distant Americans, who were known
to be rich and were generally thought, on no less
an authority than Jasper Mauduit, agent of the

Province of Massachusetts Bay, to be easily able and not unwilling to pay considerable sums towards ameliorating the revenue. It was odd, perhaps, that Americans should be willing to pay; but that was no great matter, if they were able, since no one could deny their obligation. And so country squires, and London merchants too, listened comfortably to the reading of the budget so well designed to relieve the one of taxes and swell the profits flowing into the coffers of the other.

That a duty of £2 19s. 9d. per cwt. avoirdupois, be laid upon all foreign coffee, imported from any place (except Great Britain) into the British colonies and plantations in America. That a duty of 6d. per pound weight be laid upon all foreign indico, imported into the said colonies and plantations. That a duty of £7 per ton be laid upon all wine of the growth of the Madeiras, or of any other island or place, lawfully imported from the respective place of the growth of such wine, into the said colonies and plantations. That a duty of 10s. per ton be laid upon all Portugal, Spanish, or other wine (except French wine), imported from Great Britain into the said colonies and plantations. That a duty of 2s. per pound weight be laid upon all wrought silks, Bengals, and stuffs mixed with silk or herba, of the manufacture of Persia, China, or East India, imported from Great Britain into the said colonies and plantations. That a duty of 2s. 6d. per piece be laid upon all callicoes. . . .

The list no doubt was a long one; and quite right, too, thought country squires, all of whom, to a man, were willing to pay no more land tax.

Other men besides country squires were interested in Mr. Grenville's budget, notably the West Indian sugar planters, virtually and actually represented in the House of Commons and voting there this day.   Many of them were rich men no doubt; but sugar planting, they would assure you in confidence, was not what it had been; and if they were well off after a fashion, they might have been much better off but for the shameless frauds which for thirty years had made a dead letter of the Molasses Act of 1733.   It was notorious that the merchants of the northern and middle colonies, regarding neither the Acts of Trade nor the dictates of nature, had every year carried their provisions and fish to the foreign islands, receiving in exchange molasses, cochineal, "medical druggs," and "gold and silver in bullion and coin."   With molasses the thrifty New Englanders made great quantities of inferior rum, the common drink of that day, regarded as essential to the health of sailors engaged in fishing off the Grand Banks, and by far the cheapest and most effective instrument for procuring negroes in

Africa or for inducing the western Indians to surrender their valuable furs for some trumpery of colored cloth or spangled bracelet. All this thriving traffic did not benefit British planters, who had molasses of their own and a superior quality of rum which they were not unwilling to sell.

Such traffic, since it did not benefit them, British planters were disposed to think must be bad for England. They were therefore willing to support Mr. Grenville's budget, which proposed that the importation of foreign rum into any British colony be prohibited in future; and which further proposed that the Act of 6 George II, c. 13, be continued, with modifications to make it effective, the modifications of chief importance being the additional duty of twenty-two shillings per hundredweight upon all sugar and the reduction by one half of the prohibitive duty of sixpence on all foreign molasses imported into the British plantations. It was a matter of minor importance doubtless, but one to which they had no objections since the minister made a point of it, that the produce of all the duties which should be raised by virtue of the said act, made in the sixth year of His late Majesty's reign, "be paid into the receipt of His Majesty's Exchequer, and there reserved, to be from time to time disposed of by Parliament, towards defraying the necessary expences of defending, protecting, and securing the British colonies and plantations in America."

With singularly little debate, honorable and right honorable members were ready to vote this new Sugar Act, having the minister's word for it that it would be enforced, the revenue thereby much improved, and a sudden stop put to the long-established illicit traffic with the foreign islands, a traffic so beneficial to the northern colonies, so prejudicial to the Empire and the pockets of planters. Thus it was that Mr. Grenville came opportunely to the aid of the Spanish authorities, who for many years had employed their *guarda costas* in a vain effort to suppress this very traffic, conceiving it, oddly enough, to be injurious to Spain and highly advantageous to Britain.

It may be that the Spanish authorities regarded the West Indian trade as a commercial system rather than as a means of revenue. This aspect of the matter, the commercial effects of his measures, Mr. Grenville at all events managed not to take sufficiently into account, which was rather odd, seeing that he professed to hold the commercial system embodied in the Navigation and Trade

Acts in such high esteem, as a kind of "English Palladium." No one could have wished less than Grenville to lay sacrilegious hands on this Palladium, have less intended to throw sand into the nicely adjusted bearings of the Empire's smoothly working commercial system. If he managed nevertheless to do something of this sort, it was doubtless by virtue of being such a "good man of business," by virtue of viewing the art of government too narrowly as a question of revenue only. For the moment, preoccupied as they were with the quest of revenue, the new measures seemed to Mr. Grenville and to the squires and planters who voted them well adapted to raising a moderate sum, part only of some £350,000, for the just and laudable purpose of "defraying the necessary expences of defending, protecting, and securing the British colonies and plantations in America."

The problem of colonial defense, so closely connected with the question of revenue, was none of Grenville's making but was a legacy of the war and of that Peace of Paris which had added an immense territory to the Empire. When the diplomats of England and France at last discovered, in some mysterious manner, that it had "pleased the Most High to diffuse the spirit of union and concord among the Princes," the world was informed that, as the price of "a Christian, universal, and perpetual peace," France would cede to England what had remained to her of Nova Scotia, Canada, and all the possessions of France on the left bank of the Mississippi except the City of New Orleans and the island on which it stands; that she would cede also the islands of Grenada and the Grenadines, the islands of St. Vincent, Dominica, and Tobago, and the River Senegal with all of its forts and factories; and that she would for the future be content, so far as her activities in India were concerned, with the five factories which she possessed there at the beginning of the year 1749.

The average Briton, as well as honorable and right honorable members of the House, had known that England possessed colonies and had understood that colonies, as a matter of course, existed to supply him with sugar and rice, indigo and tobacco, and in return to buy at a good price whatever he might himself wish to sell. Beyond all this he had given slight attention to the matter of colonies until the great Pitt had somewhat stirred his slow imagination with talk of empire and destiny. It was doubtless a liberalizing as well as a sobering revelation to be told that he was the "heir apparent of the Romans," with the responsibilities that are implied in having a high mission in the world. Now that his attention was called to the matter, it seemed to the average Briton that in meeting the obligation of this high mission and in dealing with this far-flung empire, a policy of efficiency such as that advocated by Mr. Grenville might well replace a policy of salutary neglect; and if the national debt had doubled during the war, as he was authoritatively assured, why indeed should not the Americans, grown rich under the fostering care of England and lately freed from the menace of France by the force of British arms, be expected to observe the Trade Acts and to contribute their fair share to the defense of that new world of which they were the chief beneficiaries?

If Americans were quite ready in their easygoing way to take chances in the matter of defense, hoping that things would turn out for the best in the future as they had in the past, British statesmen and right honorable members of the House, viewing the question broadly and without provincial illusions, understood that a policy of preparedness was the only salvation; a policy of muddling

through would no longer suffice as it had done in
the good old days before country squires and
London merchants realized that their country was
a world power. In those days, when the shrewd
Robert Walpole refused to meddle with schemes
for taxing America, the accepted theory of defense
was a simple one. If Britain policed the sea and
kept the Bourbons in their place, it was thought
that the colonies might be left to manage the Indians; fur traders, whose lure the red man could
not resist, and settlers occupying the lands beyond
the mountains, so it was said, would do the business. In 1749, five hundred thousand acres of
land had been granted to the Ohio Company
"in the King's interest" and "to cultivate a
friendship with the nations of Indians inhabiting
those parts"; and as late as 1754 the Board of
Trade was still encouraging the rapid settling of
the West, "inasmuch as nothing can more effectively tend to defeat the dangerous designs of the
French."

On the eve of the last French war it may well
have seemed to the Board of Trade that this policy
was being attended with gratifying results. In
the year 1749, La Galissonière, the acting Governor
of Canada, commissioned Céloron de Blainville to

take possession of the Ohio Valley, which he did in form, descending the river to the Maumee, and so to Lake Erie and home again, having at convenient points proclaimed the sovereignty of Louis XV over that country, and having laid down, as evidence of the accomplished fact, certain lead plates bearing awe-inspiring inscriptions, some of which have been discovered and are preserved to this day. It was none the less a dangerous junket. Everywhere Blainville found the Indians of hostile mind; everywhere, in every village almost, he found English traders plying their traffic and "cultivating a friendship with the Indians"; so that upon his return in 1750, in spite of the lead plates so securely buried, he must needs write in his journal: "All I can say is that the nations of those countries are ill disposed towards the French and devoted to the English."

During the first years of the war all this devotion was nevertheless seen to be of little worth. Like Providence, the Indians were sure to side with the big battalions. For want of a few effective garrisons at the beginning, the English found themselves deserted by their quondam allies, and although they recovered this facile allegiance as soon as the French garrisons were

taken, it was evident enough in the late years of
the war that fear alone inspired the red man's
loyalty.   The Indian apparently did not realize
at this early date that his was an inferior race destined to be supplanted.   Of a primitive and uncultivated intelligence, it was not possible for
him to foresee the beneficent designs of the Ohio
Company or to observe with friendly curiosity
the surveyors who came to draw imaginary lines
through the virgin forest.   And therefore, even in
an age when the natural rights of man were being
loudly proclaimed, the "Nations of Indians inhabiting those parts" were only too ready to believe what the Virginia traders told them of the
Pennsylvanians, what the Pennsylvania traders
told them of the Virginians — that the fair words
of the English were but a kind of mask to conceal
the greed of men who had no other desire than
to deprive the red man of his beloved hunting
grounds.

Thus it was that the industrious men with
pedantic minds who day by day read the dispatches that accumulated in the office of the
Board of Trade became aware, during the years
from 1758 to 1761, that the old policy of defense
was not altogether adequate.   "The granting of

lands hitherto unsettled," so the Board reported in 1761, "appears to be a measure of the most dangerous tendency." In December of the same year all governors were accordingly forbidden "to pass grants . . . or encourage settlements upon any lands within the said colonies which may interfere with the Indians bordering upon them."

The policy thus initiated found final expression in the famous Proclamation of 1763, in the early months of Grenville's ministry. By the terms of the Proclamation no further grants were to be made within lands "which, not having been ceded to, or purchased by us, are reserved to the said Indians" — that is to say, "all the lands lying to the westward of the sources of the rivers which fall into the sea from the west or the northwest." All persons who had "either willfully or inadvertently seated themselves" on the reserved lands were required "forthwith to remove themselves"; and for the future no man was to presume to trade with the Indians without first giving bond to observe such regulations as "we shall at any time think fit to . . . direct for the benefit of the said trade." All these provisions were designed "to the end that the Indians may be convinced of our justice and determined

resolution to remove all reasonable cause of dis-
content." By royal act the territory west of the
Alleghanies to the Mississippi, from Florida to
50° north latitude, was thus closed to settlement
"for the present" and "reserved to the Indians."

Having thus taken measures to protect the Indians against the colonists, the mother country
was quite ready to protect the colonists against
the Indians. Rash Americans were apt to say the
danger was over now that the French were "expelled from Canada." This statement was childish
enough in view of the late Pontiac uprising which
was with such great difficulty suppressed — if indeed
one could say that it was suppressed — by a general
as efficient even as Amherst, with seasoned British
troops at his command. The red man, even if
he submitted outwardly, harbored in his vengeful
heart the rankling memory of many griefs, real or
imaginary; and he was still easily swayed by his
ancient but now humiliated French friends, who
had been "expelled from Canada" only indeed in
a political sense but were still very much there as
promoters of trouble. What folly, therefore, to talk
of withdrawing the troops from America! No sane
man but could see that, under the circumstances,
such a move was quite out of the question.

It would materially change the circumstances, undoubtedly, if Americans could ever be induced to undertake, in any systematic and adequate manner, to provide for their own defense in their own way. In that case the mother country would be only too glad to withdraw her troops, of which indeed she had none too many. But it was well known what the colonists could be relied upon to do, or rather what they could be relied upon not to do, in the way of coöperative effort. Ministers had not forgotten that on the eve of the last war, at the very climax of the danger, the colonial assemblies had rejected a Plan of Union prepared by Benjamin Franklin, the one man, if any man there was, to bring the colonies together. They had rejected the plan as involving too great concentration of authority, and they were unwilling to barter the veriest jot or tittle of their much prized provincial liberty for any amount of protection. And if they rejected this plan — a very mild and harmless plan, ministers were bound to think — it was not likely they could be induced, in time of peace, to adopt any plan that might be thought adequate in England. Such a plan, for example, was that prepared by the Board of Trade, by which commissioners appointed by the governors were empowered to determine the military establish‑ ment and to apportion the expense of maintaining it among the several colonies on the basis of wealth and population. Assemblies which for years past had systematically deprived governors of all discre‑ tionary power to expend money raised by the as‑ semblies themselves would surely never surrender to governors the power of determining how much assemblies should raise for governors to expend.

Doubtless it might be said with truth that the colonies had voluntarily contributed more than their fair share in the last war; but it was also true that Pitt, and Pitt alone, could get them to do this. The King could not always count on there being in England a great genius like Pitt, and besides he did not always find it convenient, for reasons which could be given, to employ a great genius like Pitt. A system of defense had to be designed for normal times and normal men; and in normal times with normal men at the helm, ministers were agreed, the American attitude to‑ wards defense was very cleverly described by Franklin: "Everyone cries, a Union is absolutely necessary, but when it comes to the manner and form of the Union, their weak noddles are perfectly distracted."

Noddles of ministers, however, were in no way distracted but saw clearly that, if Americans could not agree on any plan of defense, there was no alternative but "an interposition of the authority of Parliament." Such interposition, recommended by the Board of Trade and already proposed by Charles Townshend in the last ministry, was now taken in hand by Grenville. The troops were to remain in America; the Mutiny Act, which required soldiers in barracks to be furnished with provisions and utensils by local authorities, and which as a matter of course went where the army went, was supplemented by the Quartering Act, which made further provision for the billeting and supplying of the troops in America. And for raising some part of the general maintenance fund ministers could think of no tax more equitable, or easier to be levied and collected, than a stamp tax. Some such tax, stamp tax or poll tax, had often been recommended by colonial governors, as a means of bringing the colonies "to a sense of their duty to the King, to awaken them to take care of their lives and their fortunes." A crown officer in North Carolina, Mr. M'Culloh, was good enough to assure Mr. Charles Jenkinson, one of the Secretaries of the Treasury, backing up his assertion with sundry statistical exhibits, that a stamp tax on the continental colonies would easily yield £60,000, and twice that sum if extended to the West Indies. As early as September 23, 1763, Mr. Jenkinson, acting on an authorization of the Treasury Board, accordingly wrote to the Commissioners of Stamped Duties, directing them "to prepare, for their Lordships' consideration, a draft of an act for imposing proper stamp duties on His Majesty's subjects in America and the West Indies."

Mr. Grenville, who was not in any case the man to do things in a hurry, nevertheless proceeded very leisurely in the matter. He knew very well that Pitt had refused to "burn his fingers" with any stamp tax; and some men, such as his friend and secretary, Mr. Jackson, for example, and the Earl of Hillsborough, advised him to abandon the project altogether, while others urged delay at least, in order that Americans might have an opportunity to present their objections, if they had any. It was decided therefore to postpone the matter for a year; and in presenting the budget on March 9, 1764, the first minister merely gave notice that "it may be proper to charge certain stamp duties in the said colonies and plantations." Of all the plans for taxing America, he said, this one seemed to him the best; yet he was not wedded to it, and would willingly adopt any other preferred by the colonists, if they could suggest any other of equal efficacy. Meanwhile, he wished only to call upon honorable members of the House to say now, if any were so minded, that Parliament had not the right to impose any tax, external or internal, upon the colonies; to which solemn question, asked in full house, there was not one negative, nor any reply except Alderman Beckford saying: "As we are stout, I hope we shall be merciful."

It soon appeared that Americans did have objections to a stamp tax. Whether it were equitable or not, they would rather it should not be laid, really preferring not to be dished up in any sauce whatever, however fine. The tax might, as ministers said, be easily collected, or its collection might perhaps be attended with certain difficulties; in either case it would remain, for reasons which they were ready to advance, a most objectionable tax. Certain colonial agents then in England accordingly sought an interview with the first minister in order to convince him, if possible, of this fact. Grenville was very likely more than ready to grant them an interview, relying upon the strength of his position, on his "tenderness for the subjects in America," and upon his well-known powers of persuasion, to bring them to his way of thinking. To get from the colonial agents a kind of assent to his measure would be to win a point of no slight strategic value, there being at least a modicum of truth in the notion that just government springs from the consent of the governed.

I have proposed the resolution [the minister explained to the agents] from a real regard and tenderness for the subjects in the colonies. It is highly reasonable they should contribute something towards the charge of protecting themselves, and in aid of the great expense Great Britain has put herself to on their account. No tax appears to me so easy and equitable as a stamp duty. It will fall only upon property, will be collected by the fewest officers, and will be equally spread over America and the West Indies. . . . It does not require any number of officers vested with extraordinary powers of entering houses, or extend a sort of influence which I never wished to increase. The colonists now have it in their power, by agreeing to this tax, to establish a precedent for their being consulted before any tax is imposed upon them by Parliament; for their approbation of it being signified to Parliament next year . . . will afford a forcible argument for the like proceeding in all such cases. If they think of any other mode of taxation more convenient to them, and make any proposition of equal efficacy with the stamp duty, I will give it all due consideration.

The agents appear at least to have been silenced by this speech, which was, one must admit, so fatherly and so very reasonable in tone; and doubtless Grenville thought them convinced, too, since he always so perfectly convinced himself. At all events, he found it possible, for this or for some other reason, to put the whole matter out of his mind until the next year. The patriotic American historian, well instructed in the importance of the Stamp Act, has at first a difficulty in understanding how it could occupy, among the things that interested English statesmen at this time, a strictly subordinate place; and he wonders greatly, as he runs with eager interest through the correspondence of Grenville for the year 1764, to find it barely mentioned there. Whether the King received him less coldly today than the day before yesterday was apparently more on the minister's mind than any possibility that the Stamp Act might be received rather warmly in the colonies. The contemporaries of Grenville, even Pitt himself, have almost as little to say about the coming great event; all of which compels the historian, reviewing the matter judiciously, to reflect sadly that Englishmen of that day were not as fully aware of the importance of the measure before it was passed as good patriots have since become.

There is much to confirm this notion in the circumstances attending the passage of the bill through Parliament in the winter of 1765. Grenville was perhaps further reassured, in spite of persistent rumors of much high talk in America, by the results of a second interview which he had with the colonial agents just before introducing the measure into the House of Commons. "I take no pleasure," he again explained in his reasonable way, "in bringing upon myself their resentments; it is my duty to manage the revenue. I have really been made to believe that, considering the whole circumstances of the mother country and the colonies, the latter can and ought to pay something to the common cause. I know of no better way than that now pursuing to lay such a tax. If you can tell of a better, I will adopt it."

Franklin, who was present with the others on this occasion, ventured to suggest that the "usual constitutional way" of obtaining colonial support, through the King's requisition, would be better. "Can you agree," asked Grenville, "on the proportions each colony should raise?" No, they could not agree, as Franklin was bound to admit, knowing the fact better than most men. And if no adequate answer was forthcoming from Franklin, a man so ready in expedients and so practiced in the subtleties of dialectic, it is no great wonder that Grenville thought the agents now fully convinced by his reasoning, which after all was only an impersonal formulation of the inexorable logic of the situation.

Proceeding thus leisurely, having taken so much pains to elicit reasonable objection and none being forthcoming, Grenville, quite sure of his ground, brought in from the Ways and Means Committee, in February, 1765, the fifty-five resolutions which required that stamped paper, printed by the government and sold by officers appointed for that purpose, be used for nearly all legal documents, for all customs papers, for appointments to all offices carrying a salary of £20 except military and judicial offices, for all grants of privilege and franchises made by the colonial assemblies, for licenses to retail liquors, for all pamphlets, advertisements, handbills, newspapers, almanacs, and calendars, and for the sale of packages containing playing cards and dice. The expediency of the act was now explained to the House, as it had been explained to the agents. That the act was legal,

which few people in fact denied, Grenville, doing
everything thoroughly and with system, proceeded
to demonstrate also.   The colonies claim, he said,
"the privilege of all British subjects of being
taxed only with their own consent."   Well, for
his part, he hoped they might always enjoy that
privilege.   "May this sacred pledge of liberty,"
cried the minister with unwonted eloquence, "be
preserved inviolate to the utmost verge of our
dominions and to the latest pages of our history."
But Americans were clearly wrong in supposing
the Stamp Act would deprive them of the rights
of Englishmen, for, upon any ground on which it
could be said that Englishmen were represented, it
could be maintained, and he was free to assert, that
Americans were represented, in Parliament, which
was the common council of the whole Empire.

The measure was well received.   Mr. Jackson
supposed that Parliament had a right to tax
America, but he much doubted the expediency of
the present act.   If it was necessary, as ministers
claimed, to tax the colonies, the latter should be
permitted to elect some part of the Parliament,
"otherwise the liberties of America, I do not say
will be lost, but will be in danger."   The one
notable event of this "slight day" was occasioned

by a remark of Charles Townshend, who asked
with some asperity whether "these American children, planted by our care, nourished up by our
indulgence to a degree of strength and opulence,
and protected by our arms," would now be so
unfilial as to "grudge to contribute their mite to
relieve us from the heavy burden under which we
lie?" Upon which Colonel Isaac Barré sprang to
his feet and delivered an impassioned, unpremedi-
tated reply which stirred the dull House for perhaps
three minutes:

They planted by *your* care! No; your oppression
planted them in America. They fled from your tyranny to a then uncultivated, inhospitable country,
where they exposed themselves to almost all the hardships to which human nature is liable. . . . They
nourished up by *your* indulgence! They grew by your
neglect of them. As soon as you began to care about
them, that care was exercised in sending persons to
rule them in one department and another, who were,
perhaps, the deputies of deputies to some members of
this house, sent to spy out their liberties, to misrepre-
sent their actions, and to prey upon them; men whose
behaviour on many occasions has caused the blood of
these sons of liberty to recoil within them. . . . They
protected by *your* arms! They have nobly taken up
arms in your defense; have exerted a valor amidst
their constant and laborious industry, for the defense
of a country whose frontier was drenched in blood,

while its interior parts yielded all its little savings to your emolument.

A very warm speech, and a capital hit, too, thought the honorable members of the House, as they settled comfortably back again to endure the routine of a dull day.   Towards midnight, after seven hours of languid debate, an adjournment was carried, as everyone foresaw it would be, by a great majority — 205 to 49 in support of the ministry.   On the 13th of February the Stamp Act bill was introduced and read for the first time, without debate.   It passed the House on the 27th; on the 8th of March it was approved by the Lords without protest, amendment, debate, or division; and two weeks later, the King being then temporarily out of his mind, the bill received the royal assent by commission.

At a later day, when the fatal effects of the Act were but too apparent, it was made a charge against the ministers that they had persisted in passing the measure in the face of strong opposition.   But it was not so.   "As to the fact of a strenuous opposition to the Stamp Act," said Burke, in his famous speech on American taxation, "I sat as a stranger in your gallery when it was under consideration.   Far from anything inflammatory, I never heard a more languid debate in this house. . . . In fact, the affair passed with so very, very little noise, that in town they scarcely knew the nature of what you were doing." So far as men concerned themselves with the doings of Parliament, the colonial measures of Grenville were greatly applauded; and that not alone by men who were ignorant of America. Thomas Pownall, once Governor of Massachusetts, well acquainted with the colonies and no bad friend of their liberties, published in April, 1764, a pamphlet on the *Administration of the Colonies* which he dedicated to George Grenville, "the great minister," who he desired might live to see the "power, prosperity, and honor that must be given to his country, by so great and important an event as the interweaving the administration of the colonies into the British administration."

4

CHAPTER III

THE RIGHTS OF A NATION

British subjects, by removing to America, cultivating a wilderness, extending the domain, and increasing the wealth, commerce, and power of the mother country, at the hazard of their lives and fortunes, ought not, and in fact do not thereby lose their native rights. — *Benjamin Franklin.*

I⊤ was the misfortune of Grenville that this "interweaving," as Pownall described it, should have been undertaken at a most inopportune time, when the very conditions which made Englishmen conscious of the burden of empire were giving to Americans a new and highly stimulating sense of power and independence. The marvelous growth of the colonies in population and wealth, much commented upon by all observers and asserted by ministers as one principal reason why Americans should pay taxes, was indeed well worth some consideration. A million and a half of people spread over the Atlantic seaboard might be thought no great number; but it was a new thing in the world.

well worth noting — which had in fact been carefully noted by Benjamin Franklin in a pamphlet on *The Increase of Mankind, Peopling of Countries, etc.* — that within three-quarters of a century the population of the continental colonies had doubled every twenty-five years, whereas the population of Old England during a hundred years past had not doubled once and now stood at only some six and a half millions.   If this should go on — and, considering the immense stretches of free land beyond the mountains, no one could suppose that the present rate of increase would soon fall off — it was not unlikely that in another century the center of empire, following the course of the sun, would come to rest in the New World.   With these facts in mind, one might indeed say that a people with so much vitality and expansive power was abundantly able to pay taxes; but perhaps it was also a fair inference, if any one was disposed to press the matter, that, unless it was so minded, such a people was already, or assuredly soon would be, equally able not to pay them.

People in new countries, being called provincial, being often told in effect that having made their bed they may lie in it, easily maintain their self-respect if they are able to say that the bed is indeed a very comfortable one. If, therefore, Americans had been given to boasting, their growing wealth was not, any more than their increasing numbers, a thing to be passed over in silence. In every colony the "starving time," even if it had ever existed, was now no more than an ancient tradition. "Every man of industry has it in his power to live well," according to William Smith of New York, "and many are the instances of persons who came here distressed in their poverty who now enjoy easy and plentiful fortunes." If Americans were not always aware that they were rich men individually, they were at all events well instructed, by old-world visitors who came to observe them with a certain air of condescension, that collectively at least their material prosperity was a thing to be envied even by more advanced and more civilized peoples. Therefore any man called upon to pay a penny tax and finding his pocket bare might take a decent pride in the fact, which none need doubt since foreigners like Peter Kalm found it so, that "the English colonies in this part of the world have increased so much in . . . their riches, that they almost vie with old England."

That the colonies might possibly "vie with old

England," was a notion which good Americans
could contemplate with much equanimity; and even
if the Swedish traveler, according to a habit of
travelers, had stretched the facts a point or two,
it was still abundantly clear that the continental
colonies were thought to be, even by Englishmen
themselves, of far greater importance to the mother
country than they had formerly been. Very old
men could remember the time when English statesmen and economists, viewing colonies as providen-
tially designed to promote the increase of trade,
had regarded the northern colonies as little better
than heavy incumbrances on the Empire, and their
commerce scarcely worth the cost of protection.
It was no longer so; it could no longer be said
that two-thirds of colonial commerce was with the
tobacco and sugar plantations, or that Jamaica
took off more English exports than the middle and
northern colonies combined; but it could be said,
and was now being loudly proclaimed — when
it was a point of debate whether to keep Canada
or Guadeloupe — that the northern colonies had
already outstripped the islands as consumers of
English commodities.

Of this fact Americans themselves were well
aware. The question whether it was for the inter-

est of England to keep Canada or Guadeloupe, which was much discussed in 1760, called forth the notable pamphlet from Franklin, entitled *The Interest of Great Britain Considered*, in which he arranged in convenient form for the benefit of Englishmen certain statistics of trade. From these statistics it appeared that, whereas in 1748 English exports to the northern colonies and to the West Indies stood at some £830,000 and £730,000 respectively, ten years later the exports to the West Indies were still no more than £877,571 while those to the northern colonies had advanced to nearly two millions. Nor was it likely that this rate of increase would fall off in the future. "The trade to our northern colonies," said Franklin, "is not only greater but yearly increasing with the increase of the people. . . . The occasion for English goods in North America, and the inclination to have and use them, is and must be for ages to come, much greater than the ability of the people to buy them." For English merchants the prospect was therefore an inviting one; and if Canada rather than Guadeloupe was kept at the close of the war, it was because statesmen and economists were coming to estimate the value of colonies in terms of what they could buy, and not merely, as of old, in terms of what they could sell. From this point of view, the superiority of the continental over the insular colonies was not to be doubted. Americans might well find great satisfaction in this disposition of the mother country to regard her continental colonies so highly and to think their trade of so much moment to her; all of which, nevertheless, doubtless inclined them sometimes to speculate on the delicate question whether, in case they were so important to the mother country, they were not perhaps more important to her than she was to them.

The consciousness of rapidly increasing material power, which was greatly strengthened by the last French war, did nothing to dull the sense of rights, but it was, on the contrary, a marked stimulus to the mind in formulating a plausible, if theoretical, justification of desired aims. Doubtless no American would say that being able to pay taxes was a good reason for not paying them, or that obligations might rightly be ignored as soon as one was in a position to do so successfully; but that he should not "lose his native rights" any American could more readily understand when he recalled that his ancestors had without assistance from the mother country transformed a wilderness into populous and thriving communities whose trade was now becoming indispensable to Britain. Therefore, in the summer of 1764, before the doctrine of colonial rights had been very clearly stated or much refined, every American knew that the Sugar Act and also the proposed Stamp Act were grievously burdensome, and that in some way or other and for reasons which he might not be able to give with precision, they involved an infringement of essential English liberties. Most men in the colonies, at this early date, would doubtless have agreed with the views expressed in a letter written to a friend in England by Thomas Hutchinson of Boston, who was later so well hated by his compatriots for not having changed his views with the progress of events.

The colonists [said Hutchinson] claim a power of making laws, and a privilege of exemption from taxes, unless voted by their own representatives. . . . Nor are the privileges of the people less affected by duties laid for the sake of the money arising from them than by an internal tax. Not one tenth part of the people of Great Britain have a voice in the elections to Parliament; and, therefore, the colonies can have no claim to it; but every man of property in England may have his voice, if he will. Besides, acts of Parliament do not generally affect individuals, and every interest is represented. But the colonies have an interest distinct from the interest of the nation; and shall the Parliament be at once party and judge? . . .

The nation treats her colonies as a father who should sell the services of his sons to reimburse him what they had cost him, but without the same reason; for none of the colonies, except Georgia and Halifax, occasioned any charge to the Crown or kingdom in the settlement of them. The people of New England fled for the sake of civil and religious liberty; multitudes flocked to America with this dependence, that their liberties should be safe. They and their posterity have enjoyed them to their content, and therefore have endured with greater cheerfulness all the hardships of settling new countries. No ill use has been made of these privileges; but the domain and wealth of Great Britain have received amazing addition. Surely the services we have rendered the nation have not subjected us to any forfeitures.

I know it is said the colonies are a charge to the nation, and they should contribute to their own defense and protection. But during the last war they annually contributed so largely that the Parliament was convinced the burden would be insupportable; and from year to year made them compensation; in several of the colonies for several years together more men were raised, in proportion, than by the nation. In the trading towns, one fourth part of the profit of trade, besides imposts and excise, was annually paid to the support of the war and public charges; in the country towns, a farm which would hardly rent for twenty pounds a year, paid ten pounds in taxes. If the inhabitants of Britain had paid in the same proportion, there would have been no great increase in the national debt.

Nor is there occasion for any national expense in America. For one hundred years together the New England colonies received no aid in their wars with the Indians, assisted by the French. Those governments now molested are as able to defend their respective frontiers; and had rather do the whole of it by a tax of their own raising, than pay their proportion in any other way. Moreover, it must be prejudicial to the national interest to impose parliamentary taxes. The advantages promised by an increase of the revenue are all fallacious and delusive. You will lose more than you will gain. Britain already reaps the profit of all their trade, and of the increase of their substance. By cherishing their present turn of mind, you will serve your interest more than by your present schemes.

Thomas Hutchinson, or any other man, might write a private letter without committing his country, or, with due caution to his correspondent, even himself; but for effective public and official protest the colonial assemblies were the proper channels, and very expert they were in the business, after having for half a century and more devoted themselves with singleness of purpose to the guardianship of colonial liberties. Until now, liberties had been chiefly threatened by the insidious designs of colonial governors, who were for the most part appointed by the Crown and very likely therefore to be infected with the spirit of prerogative than which nothing could be more dangerous, as everyone must know who recalled the great events of the last century. With those great events, the eminent men who directed the colonial assemblies — heads or scions or protégés of the best families in America, men of wealth and not without reading — were entirely familiar; they knew as well as any man that the liberties of Englishmen had been vindicated against royal prerogative only by depriving one king of his head and another of his crown; and they needed no instruction in the significance of the "glorious revolution," the high justification of which was to be found in the political gospel of John Locke, whose book they had commonly bought and conveniently placed on their library shelves.

More often than not, it is true, colonial governors were but ordinary Englishmen with neither the instinct nor the capacity for tyranny, intent mainly upon getting their salaries paid and laying by a competence against the day when they might return to England. But if they were not kings, at least they had certain royal characteristics; and a certain flavor of despotism, clinging as it were to their official robes and reviving in sensitive provincial minds the memory of bygone parliamentary battles, was an ever-present stimulus to the eternal vigilance which was well known to be the price of liberty.

And so, throughout the eighteenth century, little colonial aristocracies played their part, in imagination clothing their governors in the decaying vesture of old-world tyrants and themselves assuming the homespun garb, half Roman and half Puritan, of a virtuous republicanism. Small matters were thus stamped with great character. To debate a point of procedure in the Boston or Williamsburg assembly was not, to be sure, as high a privilege as to obstruct legislation in Westminster; but men of the best American families, fashioning their minds as well as their houses on good English models, thought of themselves, in withholding a governor's salary or limiting his executive power, as but reënacting on a lesser stage the great parliamentary struggles of the seventeenth century. It was the illusion of sharing in great events rather than any low mercenary motive that made Americans guard with jealous care their legislative independence; a certain hypersensitiveness in matters of taxation they knew to be the virtue of men standing for liberties which Englishmen had once won and might lose before they were aware.

As a matter of course, therefore, the colonial assemblies protested against the measures of Grenville. The General Court of Massachusetts instructed its agent to say that the Sugar Act would ruin the New England fisheries upon which the industrial prosperity of the northern colonies depended. What they would lose was set down with some care, in precise figures: the fishing trade, "estimated at £164,000 per annum; the vessels employed in it, which would be nearly useless, at £100,000; the provisions used in it, the casks for packing fish, and other articles, at £22,700 and upwards: to all which there was to be added the loss of the advantage of sending lumber, horses, provisions, and other commodities to the foreign plantations as cargoes, the vessels employed to carry the fish to Spain and Portugal, the dismissing of 5,000 seamen from their employment," besides many other losses, all arising from the very simple fact that the British islands to which the trade of the colonies was virtually confined by the Sugar Act could furnish no sufficient market for the products of New England, to say nothing of the middle colonies, nor a tithe of the molasses and other commodities now imported from the foreign islands in exchange.

Of the things taken in exchange, silver, in coin and bullion, was not the least important, since it was essential for the "remittances to England for goods imported into the provinces," remittances which during the last eighteen months, it was said, "had been made in specie to the amount of £150,000 besides £90,000 in Treasurer's bills for the reimbursement money." Any man must thus see, since even Governor Bernard was convinced of it, that the new duties would drain the colony of all its hard money, and so, as the Governor said, "There will be an end of the specie currency in Massachusetts." And with her trade half gone and her hard money entirely so, the old Bay colony would have to manufacture for herself those very commodities which English merchants were so desirous of selling in America.

The Sugar Act was thus made out to be, even from the point of view of English merchants, an economic blunder; but in the eyes of vigilant Bostonians it was something more, and much worse than an economic blunder. Vigilant Bostonians assembled in Town Meeting in May, 1764, in order to instruct their representatives how they ought to act in these serious times; and knowing that they ought to protest but perhaps not knowing precisely on what grounds, they committed the drafting of their instructions to Samuel Adams, a middle-aged man who had given much time to the consideration of political questions, and above all to this very question of taxation, upon which he had wonderfully clarified his ideas by much meditation and the writing of effective political pieces for the newspapers.

Through the eyes of Samuel Adams, therefore, vigilant Bostonians saw clearly that the Sugar Act, to say nothing of the Stamp Act, was not only an economic blunder but a menace to political liberty as well. "If our trade may be taxed," so the instructions ran, "why not our lands? Why not the produce of our lands, and everything we possess or make use of? This we apprehend annihilates our charter right to govern and tax ourselves. It strikes at our British privileges which, as we have never forfeited them, we hold in common with our fellow-subjects who are natives of Great Britain. If taxes are laid upon us in any shape without our having a legal representative where they are laid, are we not reduced from the character of free sub-

jects to the miserable state of tributary slaves?"
Very formidable questions, couched in high-sound-
ing phrases, and representing well enough in form
and in substance the state of mind of colonial assemblies in the summer of 1764 in respect to the
Sugar Act and the proposed Stamp Act.

Yet these resounding phrases doubtless meant
something less to Americans of 1764 than one is
apt to suppose. The rights of freemen had so
often, in the proceedings of colonial assemblies
as well as in the newspaper communications of
many a Brutus and Cato, been made to depend
upon withholding a governor's salary or defining
precisely how he should expend a hundred pounds
or so, that moderate terms could hardly be trusted
to cope with the serious business of parliamentary
taxation. "Reduced from the character of free
subjects to the miserable state of tributary slaves"
was in fact hardly more than a conventional and
dignified way of expressing a firm but entirely
respectful protest.

The truth is, therefore, that while everyone protested in such spirited terms as might occur to
him, few men in these early days supposed the new
laws would not take effect, and fewer still counseled
the right or believed in the practicability of forcible

resistance. "We yield obedience to the act granting duties," declared the Massachusetts Assembly.
"Let Parliament lay what duties they please on
us," said James Otis; "it is our duty to submit
and patiently bear them till they be pleased to
relieve us." Franklin assured his friends that the
passage of the Stamp Act could not have been
prevented any more easily than the sun's setting,
recommended that they endure the one mis-
chance with the same equanimity with which
they faced the other necessity, and even saw
certain advantages in the way of self-discipline
which might come of it through the practice of
a greater frugality. Not yet perceiving the dis-
honor attaching to the function of distributing
stamps, he did his two friends, Jared Ingersoll of
Connecticut and John Hughes of Pennsylvania,
the service of procuring for them the appointment
to the new office; and Richard Henry Lee, as
good a patriot as any man and therefore of necessity at some pains later to explain his motives in
the matter, applied for the position in Virginia.

Richard Henry Lee was no friend of tyrants,
but an American freeman, less distinguished as
yet than his name, which was a famous one and
not without offense to be omitted from any list

of the Old Dominion's "best families." The best families of the Old Dominion, tide-water tobacco planters of considerable estates, admirers and imitators of the minor aristocracy of England, took it as a matter of course that the political fortunes of the province were committed to their care and for many generations had successfully maintained the public interest against the double danger of executive tyranny and popular licentiousness. It is therefore not surprising that the many obscure freeholders, minor planters, and lesser men who filled the House of Burgesses had followed the able leadership of that little coterie of interrelated families comprising the Virginia aristocracy. John Robinson, Speaker of the House and Treasurer of the colony, of good repute still in the spring of 1765, was doubtless the head and front of this aristocracy, the inner circle of which would also include Peyton Randolph, then King's Attorney, and Edmund Pendleton, well known for his cool persuasiveness in debate, the learned constitutional lawyer, Richard Bland, the sturdy and honest but ungraceful Robert Carter Nicholas, and George Wythe, noblest Roman of them all, steeped in classical lore, with the thin, sharp face of a Cæsar and for virtuous integrity a very

Cato. Conscious of their English heritage, they were at once proud of their loyalty to Britain and jealous of their well-won provincial liberties. As became British-American freemen, they had already drawn a proper Memorial against the Sugar Act and were now, as they leisurely gathered at Williamsburg in the early weeks of May, 1765, unwilling to protest again at present, for they had not as yet received any reply to their former dignified and respectful petition.

To this assembly of the burgesses in 1765, there came from the back-country beyond the first falls of the Virginia rivers, the frontier of that day, many deputies who must have presented, in dress and manners as well as in ideas, a sharp contrast to the eminent leaders of the aristocracy. Among them was Thomas Marshall, father of a famous son, and Patrick Henry, a young man of twenty-nine years, a heaven-born orator and destined to be the leader and interpreter of the silent "simple folk" of the Old Dominion. In Hanover County, in which this tribune of the people was born and reared and which he now represented, there were, as in all the back-country counties, few great estates and few slaves, no notable country-seats with pretension to archi-

tectural excellence, no modishly dressed aristocracy with leisure for reading and the cultivation
of manners becoming a gentleman. Beyond the
tide-water, men for the most part earned their
bread by the sweat of their brows, lived the life
and esteemed the virtues of a primitive society,
and braced their minds with the tonic of Calvin's
theology — a tonic somewhat tempered in these
late enlightened days by a more humane philo-
sophy and the friendly emotionalism of simple folk
living close to nature.

Free burgesses from the back-country, set apart
in dress and manners from the great planters, less
learned and less practiced in oratory and the subtle
art of condescension and patronage than the cultivated men of the inner circle, were nevertheless
staunch defenders of liberty and American rights
and were perhaps beginning to question, in these
days of popular discussion, whether liberty could
very well flourish among men whose wealth was
derived from the labor of negro slaves, or be well
guarded under all circumstances by those who, regarding themselves as superior to the general run
of men, might be in danger of mistaking their particular interests for the common welfare.   And indeed it now seemed that these great men who sent

their sons to London to be educated, who every year shipped their tobacco to England and bought their clothes of English merchants with whom their credit was always good, were grown something too timid, on account of their loyalty to Britain, in the great question of asserting the rights of America.

Jean Jacques Rousseau would have well understood Patrick Henry, one of those passionate temperaments whose reason functions not in the service of knowledge but of good instincts and fine emotions; a nature to be easily possessed of an exalted enthusiasm for popular rights and for celebrating the virtues of the industrious poor.   This enthusiasm in the case of Patrick Henry was intensified by his own eloquence, which had been so effectively exhibited in the famous Parson's Cause, and in opposition to the shady scheme which the old leaders in the House of Burgesses had contrived to protect John Robinson, the Treasurer, from being exposed to a charge of embezzlement.   Such courageous exploits, widely noised abroad, had won for the young man great applause and had got him a kind of party of devoted followers in the back-country and among the yeomanry and young men throughout the province, so that to take the lead and to stand boldly forth as the champion of liberty and the submerged rights of mankind seemed to Patrick Henry a kind of mission laid upon him, in virtue of his heavenly gift of speech, by that Providence which shapes the destinies of men.

It was said that Mr. Henry was not learned in the law; but he had read in *Coke upon Littleton* that an Act of Parliament against Magna Carta, or common right, or reason, is void — which was clearly the case of the Stamp Act. On the flyleaf of an old copy of that book this unlearned lawyer accordingly wrote out some resolutions of protest which he showed to his friends, George Johnston and John Fleming, for their approval. Their approval once obtained, Mr. Johnston moved, with Mr. Henry as second, that the House of Burgesses should go into committee of the whole, "to consider the steps necessary to be taken in consequence of the resolutions . . . charging certain Stamp Duties in the colonies"; which was accordingly done on the 29th of May, upon which day Mr. Henry presented his resolutions.

The 29th of May was late in that session of the Virginia House of Burgesses; and most likely the resolutions would have been rejected if some two-thirds of the members, who knew nothing of Mr. Henry's plans and supposed the business of the

Assembly finished, had not already gone home.
Among those who had thus departed, it is not
likely that there were many of Patrick Henry's followers. Yet even so there was much opposition.
The resolutions were apparently refashioned in
committee of the whole, for a preamble was omitted outright and four "Resolves" were made over
into five which were presented to the House on
the day following.

Young Mr. Jefferson, at that time a law student
and naturally much interested in the business of
lawmaking, heard the whole of this day's famous
debate from the door of communication between
the House and the lobby. The five resolutions, he
afterwards remembered, were "opposed by Randolph, Bland, Pendleton, Nicholas, Wythe, and
all the old members, whose influence in the House
had, till then, been unbroken; . . . not from any
question of our rights, but on the ground that
the same sentiments had been, at their preceding
session, expressed in a more conciliatory form,
to which the answers were not yet received. But
torrents of sublime eloquence from Mr. Henry,
backed by the solid reasoning of Johnston, prevailed." It was in connection with the fifth resolution, upon which the debate was "most bloody,"

that Patrick Henry is said to have declared
that "Tarquin and Cæsar had each his Brutus,
Charles the First his Cromwell, and George the
Third—"; upon which cries of "Treason" were
heard from every part of the House. Treason or
not, the resolution was carried, although by one
vote only; and the young law student standing at
the door of the House heard Peyton Randolph say,
as he came hastily out into the lobby: "By God,
I would have given 500 guineas for a single vote."
And no doubt he would, at that moment, being
then much heated.

Next day Mr. Randolph was probably much
cooler; and so apparently were some others who,
in the enthusiasm of debate and under the compel-
ling eye of Patrick Henry, had voted for the last
defiant resolution. Thinking the matter settled,
Patrick Henry had already gone home "to recommend himself to his constituents," as his enemies
thought, "by spreading treason."

But the matter was not yet settled. Early on
that morning of the 31st, before the House assembled, the young law student who was so curious
about the business of lawmaking saw Colonel Peter
Randolph, of his Majesty's Council, standing at the
Clerk's table, "thumbing over the volumes of jour-

nals to find a precedent for expunging a vote of
the House." Whether the precedent was found
the young law student did not afterwards recol-
lect; but it is known that on motion of Peyton
Randolph the fifth resolution was that day erased
from the record. Mr. Henry was not then present.
He had been seen, on the afternoon before, "passing
along the street, on his way to his home in Louisa,
clad in a pair of leather breeches, his saddle-bags on
his arm, leading a lean horse."

The four resolutions thus adopted as the deliberate and formal protest of the Old Dominion were
as mild and harmless as could well be. They
asserted no more than that the first adventurers
and settlers of Virginia brought with them and
transmitted to their posterity all the privileges
at any time enjoyed by the people of Great Britain; that by two royal charters they had been
formally declared to be as surely possessed of
these privileges as if they had been born and were
then abiding within the realm; that the taxation
of the people by themselves or by persons chosen
by themselves to represent them "is the only
security against a burthensome taxation, and the
distinguishing characteristick of British freedom,
without which the ancient constitution cannot

exist"; and that the loyal colony of Virginia had
in fact without interruption enjoyed this ines-
timable right, which had never been forfeited
or surrendered nor ever hitherto denied by the
kings or the people of Britain. No treason here,
expressed or implied; nor any occasion for 500
guineas passing from one hand to another to prove
that the province of Virginia was still the ancient
and loyal Old Dominion.

But Fate, or Providence, or whatever it is that
presides at the destinies of nations, has a way of
setting aside with ironical smile the most deliberate actions of men. And so, on this occasion,
it turned out that the hard-won victory of Messrs.
Randolph, Bland, Pendleton, and Wythe was of
no avail. William Gordon tells us, without men-
tioning the source of his information, that "a manuscript of the unrevised resolves soon reached Philadelphia, having been sent off immediately upon
their passing, that the earliest information of what
had been done might be obtained by the Sons of
Liberty." From Philadelphia a copy was for-
warded, on June 17, to New York, in which loyal
city the resolutions were thought "so treasonable
that their possessors declined printing them"; but
an Irish gentleman from Connecticut, who was

then in town, inquired after them and was with great precaution permitted to take a copy, which he straightway carried to New England. All this may be true or not; but certain it is that six resolutions purporting to come from Virginia were printed in the Newport *Mercury* on June 24, 1765, and afterwards, on July 1, in many Boston papers.

The document thus printed did not indeed include the famous fifth resolution upon which the debate in the House of Burgesses was "most bloody" and which had been there adopted by a single vote and afterwards erased from the record; but it included two others much stronger than that eminently treasonable one:

Resolved, That his Majesty's Liege people, the inhabitants of this colony, are not bound to yield obedience to any law or ordinance whatever, designed to impose any taxation whatsoever upon them, other than the laws and ordinances of the General Assembly aforesaid.   *Resolved*, That any person who shall, by speaking or writing, assert or maintain that any person or persons, other than the General Assembly of this colony, have any right or power to impose any taxation on the people here, shall be deemed an enemy to his Majesty's colony.

These resolutions, which Governor Fauquier had not seen, and which were perhaps never debated in the House of Burgesses, were now circulated far and wide as part of the mature decision of the Virginia Assembly. On the 14th of September, Messrs. Randolph, Wythe, and Nicholas were appointed a committee to apprise the Assembly's agent "of a spurious copy of the resolves of the last Assembly . . . being dispersed and printed in the News Papers and to send him a true copy of the votes on that occasion." In those days of slow and difficult communication, the truth, three months late, could not easily overtake the falsehood or ever effectively replace it.

In later years, when it was thought an honor to have begun the Revolution, many men denied the decisive effect of the Virginia Resolutions in convincing the colonists that the Stamp Act might be successfully resisted. But contemporaries were agreed in according them that glory or that infamy. "Two or three months ago," said Governor Bernard, "I thought that this people would submit to the Stamp Act. Murmurs were indeed continually heard, but they seemed to be such as would die away. The publishing the Virginia Resolutions proved an alarm-bell to the disaffected." We read the resolutions, said Jonathan Sewell, "with wonder. They savored of independence; they flattered the human passions; the reasoning was specious; we wished it conclusive. The transition to believing it so was easy, and we, almost all America, followed their example in resolving that the Parliament had no such right." And the good patriot John Adams, who afterwards attributed the honor to James Otis, said in 1776 that the "author of the first Virginia Resolutions against the Stamp Act . . . will have the glory with posterity of beginning . . . this great Revolution."[1]

James Otis in 1765 declared the Virginia Resolutions to be treasonable. It was precisely their treasonable flavor that electrified the country, while the fact that they came from the Old Dominion made men think that a union of the colonies, so essential to successful resistance, might

---

[1] Upon the death of George II., 1760, the collectors of the customs at Boston applied for new writs of assistance. The grant was opposed by the merchants, and the question was argued before the Superior Court. It was on this occasion that James Otis made a speech in favor of the rights of the colonists as men and Englishmen. All that is known of it is contained in some rough notes taken at the time by John Adams (*Works of John Adams*, ii., 125). An elaboration of these notes was printed in the Massachusetts *Spy*, April 29, 1773, and with corrections by Adams fifty years after the event in William Tudor's *Life of James Otis*, chs. 5–7. This is the speech to which Adams, at a later date, attributed the beginning of the Revolution.

be achieved in spite of all. The Old Dominion, counted the most English of the colonies in respect to her institutions and her sympathies, had a character for loyalty that, in any matter of opposition to Britain, gave double weight to her action. Easy-going tobacco-planters, Church of England men all, were well known not to be great admirers of the precise Puritans of New England, whose moral fervor and conscious rectitude seemed to them a species of fanaticism savoring more of canting hypocrisy than of that natural virtue affected by men of parts. Franklin may well have had Virginia and Massachusetts in mind when he said, but a few years earlier, no one need fear that the colonies "will unite against their own nation . . . which 'tis well known they all love much more than they love one another." Nor could anyone have supposed that the "Ancient and Loyal Colony of Virginia" would out-Boston Boston in asserting the rights of America. Yet this was what had come to pass, the evidence of which was the printed resolutions now circulating far and wide and being read in this month of July when it was being noised about that a Congress was proposed for the coming October. The proposal had in fact come from Massachusetts.

Bay in the form of a circular letter inviting all the colonies to send delegates to New York for the purpose of preparing a loyal and humble "representation of their condition," and of imploring relief from the King and Parliament of Great Britain.

No very encouraging response was immediately forthcoming. The Assembly of New Jersey unanimously declined to send any delegates, although it declared itself "not without a just sensibility respecting the late acts of Parliament," and wished "such other colonies as think proper to be active every success they can loyally and reasonably desire." For two months there was no indication that any colony would think it "proper to be active"; but during August and September the assemblies of six colonies chose deputies to the congress, and when that body finally assembled in October, less formally designated representatives from three other colonies appeared upon the scene. The Assembly of New Hampshire declined to take part. Virginia, Georgia, and North Carolina were also unrepresented, which was perhaps due to the fact that the governors of those provinces refused to call the assemblies together to consider the Massachusetts circular letter.

Of the 27 members of the Stamp Act Congress, few if any were inclined to rash or venturesome measures. It is reported that Lord Melbourne, as Prime Minister of England, once remarked to his Cabinet, "It doesn't matter what we say, but we must all say the same thing." What the Stamp Act Congress said was to be sure of some importance, but that it should say something which all could agree to was of even greater importance. "There ought to be no New England man, no New Yorker, known on the continent," wrote Christopher Gadsden of South Carolina, "but all of us Americans." New Yorkers and New England men could not indeed be so easily transformed over night; but the Stamp Act Congress was significant as marking a kind of beginning in that slow and difficult process. After eleven days of debate, in which sharp differences of opinion were no doubt revealed, a declaration of rights and grievances was at last adopted; a declaration which was so cautiously and loyally phrased that all could subscribe to it, and which was perhaps for that very reason not quite satisfactory to anyone.

His Majesty's subjects in the colonies, the declaration affirmed, are entitled to those "inherent rights and liberties" which are enjoyed by "his natural born subjects" in Great Britain; among which rights is that most important one of "not being taxed without their own consent"; and since the people of the colonies, "from local circumstances, cannot be represented in the House of Commons," it follows that taxes cannot be "imposed upon them, but by their respective legislatures." The Stamp Act, being a direct tax, was therefore declared to have a "manifest tendency to subvert the rights and liberties of the colonies." Of the Sugar Act, which was not a direct tax, so much could not be said; but this act was at least "burthensome and grievous," being subversive of trade if not of liberty. No one was likely to be profoundly stirred by the declaration of the Stamp Act Congress, in this month of October when the spirited Virginia Resolutions were everywhere well known.

"The frozen politicians of a more northern government," according to the *Boston Gazette*, "say they [the people of Virginia] have spoken treason"; but the *Boston Gazette*, for its part, thought they had "spoken very sensibly." With much reading of the resolutions and of the commendatory remarks with which they were everywhere received, the treasonable flavor of their boldest phrases no doubt grew less pronounced, and high talk took on more and more the character of good sense. During the summer of 1765 the happy phrase of Isaac Barré — "these sons of liberty" — was everywhere repeated, and was put on as a kind of protective coloring by strong patriots, who henceforth thought of themselves as Sons of Liberty and no traitors at all. Rather were they traitors who would in any way justify an act of tyranny; most of all those so-called Americans, accepting the office of Stamp Master, who cunningly aspired to make a farthing profit out of the hateful business of enslaving their own countrymen.

Who these gentry might be was not certainly known until early August, when Jared Ingersoll, himself as it turned out one of the miscreants, brought the commissions over from London, whereupon the names were all printed in the papers. It then appeared that the gentleman appointed to distribute the stamps in Massachusetts was Andrew Oliver, a man very well connected in that province and of great influence with the best people, not infrequently entrusted with high office and perquisites, and but recently elected by the unsuspecting Bostonians to represent them in the council of Massachusetts Bay Colony. It seemed inconsistent that a man so often honored by the people should meanwhile pledge himself to destroy their liberties; and so on the morning of the 14th of August, Mr. Oliver's effigy, together with a horned devil's head peeping out of an old boot, was to be seen hanging from the Liberty Tree at the south end of Boston, near the distillery of Thomas Chase, brewer and warm Son of Liberty. During the day people stopped to make merry over the spectacle; and in the evening, after work hours, a great crowd gathered to see what would happen. When the effigy was cut down and carried away, the crowd very naturally followed along through the streets and through the Town House, justifying themselves — many respectable people were in the crowd — for being there by calling out, "Liberty and Property forever; no Stamp." And what with tramping and shouting in the warm August evening, the whole crowd became much heated and ever more enthusiastic, so that, the line of march by some chance lying past the new stamp office and Mr. Oliver's house, the people were not to be restrained from destroying the former and breaking in the windows of the latter, in detestation of the hated Stamp Act and of the principle that property might be taken without consent.

Mr. Oliver hastened to resign his office, which doubtless led many people to think the methods taken to induce him to do so were very good ones and such as might well be made further use of. It was in fact not long afterwards, about dusk of the evening of the 26th of August, that a mob of men, more deliberately organized than before, ransacked the office of William Story, Deputy Registrar of the Court of Admiralty, and, after burning the obnoxious records kept there, they forcibly entered the house, and the cellar too, of Benjamin Hallowell, Comptroller of the Customs. "Then the Monsters," says Deacon Tudor, "being enflam'd with Rum & Wine which they got in sd. Hallowell's cellar, proceeded with Shouts to the Dwelling House of the Hon-l. Thos. Hutchinson, Esq., Lieut. Governor, & enter'd in a voyalent manner." At that moment the Lieutenant-Governor was sitting comfortably at dinner and had barely time to escape with his family before the massive front door was broken in with axes. As young Mr. Hutchinson went out by the back way he heard someone say: "Damn him, he's upstairs, we'll have him yet." They did not indeed accomplish this purpose; but when the morning broke the splendid house was seen to be completely gutted, the partition walls broken in, the roof partly off, and the priceless possessions of the owner ruined past repair: mahogany and walnut furniture finished in morocco and crimson damask, tapestries and Turkey carpets, rare paintings, cabinets of fine glass and old china, stores of immaculate linen, India paduasoy gowns and red Genoa robes, a choice collection of books richly bound in leather and many manuscript documents, the fruit of thirty years' labor in collecting — all broken and cut and cast about to make a rubbish heap and a bonfire. From the mire of the street there was afterwards picked up a manuscript history of Massachusetts which is preserved to this day, the soiled pages of which may still be seen in the Boston library. Mr. Hutchinson was no friend of the Stamp Act; but he was a rich man, Lieutenant-Governor of the province, and brother-in-law of Andrew Oliver.

Government offered the usual rewards — which were never claimed — for evidence leading to the detection of any persons concerned in the riots. Men of repute, including the staunchest patriots such as Samuel Adams and Jonathan Mayhew, expressed their abhorrence of mobs and of all licentious proceedings in general; but many were nevertheless disposed to think, with good Dea con Tudor, that in this particular instance "the universal Obhorrance of the Stamp Act was the cause of the Mob's riseing." It would be well to punish the mob, but punishing the mob would not cure the evil which was the cause of the mob; for where there was oppression the lower sort of people, as was well known, would be sure to express opposition in the way commonly practiced by them everywhere, in London as well as in Boston, by gathering in the streets in crowds, in which event some deplorable excesses were bound to follow, however much deprecated by men of substance and standing. If ministers wished the people to be tranquil, let them repeal the Stamp Act; if they were determined to persist in it, and should attempt to land and distribute the stamps, loyal and law-abiding citizens, however much they might regret the fact, could only say that similar disorders were very likely to become even more frequent and more serious in the future than they had been in the past.

As the first of November approached, that being the day set for the levying of the tax, attention and discussion came naturally to center on the stamps rather than on the Stamp Act. Crowds of curious people gathered wherever there seemed a prospect of catching a glimpse of the bundles of stamped papers. Upon their arrival the papers had to be landed; they could therefore be seen; and the mere sight of them was likely to be a sufficient challenge to action. It seemed a simple matter to resist a law which could be of no effect without the existence of certain papers, paper being a substance easily disposed of. And everywhere in fact the stamps were disposed of — disposed of by mobs, with the tacit consent and impalpable encouragement of many men who, having a reputable position to maintain, would themselves by no means endure to be seen in a common crowd; men of good estate whom no one could think of as countenancers of violence, but who were, on this occasion, as Mr. Livingston said, "not averse to a little rioting" on condition that it be kept within bounds and well directed to the attainment of their just rights.

A little rioting, so easy to be set on foot, was difficult to keep within reasonable bounds, as Mr. Livingston and his friends in New York soon discovered, somewhat to their chagrin. In New York, even after the stamps were surrendered by Lieutenant-Governor Colden and safely lodged in the

Town House, there were many excesses wholly un-
necessary to the attainment of the original object.
Mr. Colden's new chariot, certainly never designed
to carry the stamps, was burned; and on repeated
occasions windows were broken and "particulars"
threatened that their houses would presently be
pulled down. Mr. Livingston was himself the
owner of houses, had an immense respect for property rights and for the law that guaranteed them,
and therefore wished very much that the lower
sort of people would give over their mobbish practices now that the stamps had been disposed of.
Since the law could not now operate without
stamps, what more was necessary except to wait
in good order, patiently denying themselves those
activities that involved a violation of the law,
until the law should be repealed? The Stamp Act
Congress had protested in a proper and becoming manner; merchants had agreed not to import
British goods; the Governor had closed the courts.
Stopping of business would doubtless be annoy-
ing and might very likely produce some distress.
But it would be legal and it would be effective:
the government would get no revenue; British
merchants no profit; and Americans could not be
charged with violating a law the failure of which

was primarily due to the fact that papers indispensable to its application were, for one reason or another, not forthcoming.

Mr. Livingston, happily possessed of the conservative temperament, was disposed to achieve desired ends with the least possible disturbance of his own affairs and those of his country; and most men of independent means, landowners and merchants of considerable estates, moneyed men and high salaried officials whose incomes were not greatly affected by any temporary business depression, were likely to be of Mr. Livingston's opinion, particularly in this matter of the Stamp Act. Sitting comfortably at dinner every day and well knowing where they could lay hands on money to pay current bills, they enjoyed a high sense of being defenders of liberty and at the same time eminently law-abiding citizens. They professed a decided preference for nullifying the Stamp Act without violating it. Sitting at dinner over their wine, they swore that they would let ships lie in harbor and rot there if necessary, and would let the courts close for a year or two years, rather than employ taxed papers to collect their just debts; with a round oath they bound themselves to it, sealing the pledge, very likely, by sipping another glass of Madeira. In the defense of just rights, Mr. Livingston and his conservative friends were willing to sacrifice much: they foresaw some months of business stagnation, which they nevertheless contemplated with equanimity, being prepared to tide over the dull time by living in a diminished manner, if necessary even dispensing with customary bottles of Madeira at dinner.

Men of radical temperament, having generally less regard for the *status quo*, are quick to see ulterior motives back of conservative timidity and solemn profession of respect for law and order. It was so in the case of the Stamp Act. Small shopkeepers who were soon sold out and had no great stock of "old moth-eaten goods" to offer at enhanced prices, rising young lawyers whose fees ceased with the closing of the courts, artisans and laborers who bought their dinners (no Madeira included) with their daily wage — these, and indeed all the lower sort of people, contemplated the stopping of business with much alarm Mr. John Adams, a young lawyer of Braintree and Boston, was greatly interested in the question of the courts of justice. Were the courts to be closed on the ground that no legal business could be done without stamped papers? Or were they to go on trying cases, enforcing the collection of debts, and probating wills precisely as if no Stamp Act had ever been heard of?   The Boston superior court was being adjourned continuously, for a fortnight at a time, through the influence of Messrs. Hutchinson and Oliver, to the great and steadily rising wrath of young Mr. Adams.   The courts must soon be opened, he said to himself; their inactivity "will make a large chasm in my affairs, if it should not reduce me to distress." Young Mr. Adams, who had, no less than Mr. Oliver, a family to support and children to provide for, was just at the point of making a reputation and winning a competence "when this execrable project was set on foot for my ruin as well as that of America in general."   And therefore Mr. Adams, and Mr. Samuel Adams, and Mr. Otis, and Mr. Gridley, in order to avert the ruin of America in general, were "very warm" to have the courts open and very bitter against Messrs. Hutchinson and Oliver whose "insolence and impudence and chicanery" in the matter were obvious, and whose secret motives might easily be inferred.   Little wonder if these men, who had managed by hook or crook to get into their own hands or into the hands of their families nearly all the lucrative

offices in the province, now sought to curry favor
with ministers in order to maintain their amazing
ascendancy!

When the Stamp Act was passed, all men in America had professed themselves, and were thought to
be, Sons of Liberty. Even Mr. Hutchinson had
declared himself against ministerial measures. But
scarce a month had elapsed since the law was to
have gone into effect before it was clear to the discerning that, for all their professions, most of the
"better sort" were not genuine Sons of Liberty
at all, but timid sycophants, pliant instruments
of despotism, far more intent upon the ruin of Mr.
Adams and of America in general than any minister could be shown to be. For the policy of dispensing with activities requiring stamped papers,
much lauded by these gentry as an effective and
constitutional means of defeating the law, was
after all nothing but "a sort of admittance of the
legality of the Stamp Act, and had a tendency to
enforce it, since there was just reason to apprehend that the secret enemies of liberty had actually
a design to introduce it by the necessity to which
the people would be reduced by the cessation of
business." It was well, therefore, in view of such
insidious designs of secret enemies, that the people,

even to the lowest ranks, should become "more attentive to their liberties, and more inquisitive about them, and more determined to defend them, than they were ever before known or had occasion to be."

To defend their liberties, not against ministers but against ministerial tools, who were secret betrayers of America, true patriots accordingly banded themselves in societies which took to themselves the name of Sons of Liberty and of which the object was, by "putting business in motion again, in the usual channels, without stamps," to prevent the Stamp Act ever being enforced. Such a society composed mainly of the lower orders of people and led by rising young lawyers, was formed in New York   On January 7, at Mr. Howard's coffee house, abandoning the secrecy which had hitherto veiled their activities, its members declared to the world their principles and the motives that would determine their action in the future:

Resolved: That we will go to the last extremity and venture our lives and fortunes effectively to prevent the said Stamp Act from ever taking place in this city and province; *Resolved:* That any person who shall deliver out or receive any instrument of writing upon stamped paper . . . shall incur the highest resentment of this society, and be branded with everlasting infamy; *Resolved:* That the people who carry on business as formerly on unstamped paper . . . shall be protected to the utmost power of this society.

Malicious men said that the Sons of Liberty were "much concerned that the gentlemen of fortune don't publically join them," for which reason the society "formed a committee of correspondence with the Liberty Boys in the neighboring provinces."   In February, the society did in fact appoint such a committee, which sent out letters to all the counties of New York and to all the colonies except Georgia, proposing the formation of an intercolonial association of the true Sons of Liberty; to which letters many replies were received, some of which are still preserved among the papers of the secretary, Mr. John Lamb.   The general sense of these letters was that an intercolonial association and close correspondence were highly necessary in view of the presence, in nearly every colony, of many "secret and inveterate enemies of liberty," and of the desirability of keeping "a watchful eye over all those who, from the nature of their offices, vocations, or dispositions, may be the most likely to introduce the use of stamped paper, to the total subversion of the British constitution."

No doubt the society kept its watchful eye on every unusual activity and all suspicious characters, but to what extent it succeeded in "putting business in motion again, in the usual channels, without stamps," cannot be said. Both before and after the society was founded, much business was carried on in violation of the law: newspapers and pamphlets continued to flourish in the land; the inferior courts at least were sooner or later opened in nearly every colony; and not infrequently unstamped clearance papers were issued to shipmasters willing to take the risk of seizure in London or elsewhere. Mr. John Hancock, easily persuading himself that there should be no risk, shipped a cargo of oil with the Boston packet in December. "I am under no apprehensions," he wrote his London agent. "Should there be any Difficulty in London as to Marshall's clearance, You will please to represent the circumstances that no stamps could be obtained, . . . in which case I think I am to be justified, & am not liable to a seizure, or even run any risque at all, as I have taken the Step of the Law, and made application for clearance, & can get no other."

Notwithstanding such practices, which were frequent enough, it was a dull winter, with little profit flowing into the coffers of Mr. Hancock, with low wages or none at all for worthy artisans and laborers; so that it must often have seemed, as Governor Moore said, "morally impossible that the people here can subsist any time under such inconveniences as they have brought on themselves." Such inconveniences became more irksome as time passed, with the result that, during the cold and dreary months of February and March, it became every day a more pressing question, particularly for the poor, to know whether the bad times would end at last in the repeal or the admission of the tyrannical act.

Confronted with this difficult dilemma, the faithful Sons of Liberty were preparing in April to assemble a continental congress as a last resort, when rumors began to spread that Parliament was on the point of carrying the repeal. The project of a congress was accordingly abandoned, and everywhere recrimination gave place to rejoicing. On April 21, 1766, the vigilant Boston Sons voted that when the rumors should be confirmed they would celebrate the momentous event in a befitting manner — would celebrate it "Under the deepest Sense of Duty and Loyalty to our Most Gracious Sovereign King George, and in respect

and Gratitude to the Patriotic Ministry, Mr.
Pitt, and the Glorious Majority of both Houses
of Parliament, by whose Influence, under Divine
Providence, against a most strenuous Opposition,
a happy Repeal of the Stamp Act, so unconstitutional as well as Grievous to His Majesty's good
Subjects of America, is attained; whereby our
incontestible Right of Internal Taxation remains
to us inviolate."

7

CHAPTER IV

DEFINING THE ISSUE

A pepper-corn, in acknowledgement of the right, is of more value than millions without it. — *George Grenville.*

A perpetual jealousy respecting liberty, is absolutely requisite in all free states. — *John Dickinson.*

GOOD Americans everywhere celebrated the repeal of the Stamp Act with much festivity and joyful noises in the streets, and with "genteel entertainments" in taverns, where innumerable toasts were drunk to Liberty and to its English defenders. Before his house on Beacon Hill, Mr. John Hancock, on occasion a generous man, erected a platform and placed there a pipe of Madeira which was broached for all comers. At Colonel Ingersoll's, where twenty-eight gentlemen attended to take dinner, fifteen toasts were drunk, "and very loyal they were, and suited to the occasion"; upon which occasion, we are told, Mr. Hancock again "treated every person with cheerfulness." Throughout the land men with literary gifts, or instincts, delivered themselves of vigorous free verse, founded upon the antithesis of Freedom and Tyranny, and enforcing the universal truth that "in the unequal war Oppressors fall, the hate, contempt, and endless curse of all." In New York, on the occasion of the King's birthday, an ox was roasted whole in the Fields, and twenty kegs of beer were opened for a great dinner at the King's Arms; and afterwards, through the generosity of the Assembly of that province, there was erected on the Bowling Green a mounted statue — made of lead but without present intention of being turned into bullets — representing His Majesty King George the Third, of ever glorious memory, the Restorer of Liberty.

The joyful Americans could not know how little King George aspired to be thought the Restorer of Liberty. In reality he was extremely sulky in his silent, stubborn way over the repeal of the Stamp Act, and vexed most particularly at the part which he himself had been forced to play in it. The idea of a Patriot King, conceived by Lord Bolingbroke (one-time Jacobite exile) and instilled into the mind of the young Hanoverian monarch by an ambitious mother, had little to do with liberty, either British or colonial, but had much to do with authority. The Patriot King was to be a king indeed, seeking advice of all virtuous men of whatever connections, without being bound by any man or faction of men. It was not to restore liberty, nor yet to destroy it, but to destroy factions, that the King was ambitious; and for this purpose he desired a ministry that would do his bidding without too much question. If Mr. Grenville did not satisfy His Majesty, it was not on account of the Stamp Act, in respect to which the King was wholly of Mr. Grenville's opinion that it was a just law and ought to be enforced. In July, 1765, when Mr. Grenville was dismissed, there had indeed as yet been no open resistance in America; and if the King had been somewhat annoyed by the high talk of his loyal subjects in Virginia, he had been annoyed much more by Mr. Grenville, who was disposed, in spite of his outward air of humility and solemn protestations of respect, to be very firm with His Majesty in the matter of ministerial prerogative, reading him from time to time carefully prepared pedantic little curtain lectures on the customs of the Constitution and the duties of kings under particular circumstances.

Unable to endure Mr. Grenville longer, the King

turned to Mr. Pitt. This statesman, although extremely domineering in the House, was much subdued in the presence of his sovereign, and along with many defects had one great virtue in his Majesty's eyes, which was that he shared the King's desire to destroy the factions. The King was accordingly ready to receive the Great Commoner, even though he insisted on bringing "the Constitution," and Earl Temple into the bargain, with him to St. James's Palace. But when it appeared that Earl Temple was opposed to the repeal of the Stamp Act, Mr. Pitt declined after all to come to St. James's on any terms, even with his beloved Constitution; whereupon the harassed young King, rather than submit again to Mr. Grenville's lectures, surrendered himself, temporarily, to the old-line Whigs under the lead of the Marquis of Rockingham. In all the negotiations which ended in this unpromising arrangement of the King's business, the Stamp Act had apparently not been once mentioned; except that Mr. Grenville, upon retiring, had ventured to say to His Majesty, as a kind of abbreviated parting homily, that if "any man ventured to defeat the regulations laid down for the colonies, by a slackness in the execution, he [Mr. Grenville] should look upon him as a criminal and the betrayer of his country."

The Marquis of Rockingham and his friends had no intention of betraying their country. They had, perhaps, when they were thus accidentally lifted to power, no very definite intentions of any sort. Respecting the Stamp Act, as most alarming reports began to come in from America, His Majesty's Opposition, backed by the landed interest and led by Mr. Grenville and the Duke of Bedford, knew its mind much sooner than ministers knew theirs. America was in open rebellion, they said, and so far from doing anything about it ministers were not even prepared, four months after disturbances began, to lay necessary information before the House. Under pressure of such talk, the Marquis of Rockingham had to make up his mind. It would be odd and contrary to well-established precedent for ministers to adopt a policy already outlined by Opposition; and in view of the facts that good Whig tradition, even if somewhat obscured in latter days, committed them to some kind of liberalism, that the City and the mercantile interest thought Mr. Grenville's measures disastrous to trade, and that they were much in need of Mr. Pitt's eloquence to carry them through, ministers at last, in January, 1766, declared for the repeal.

Now that it was a question of repealing Mr. Grenville's measures, serious attention was given to them; and honorable members, in the notable debate of 1766, learned much about America and the rights of Englishmen which they had not known before. Lord Mansfield, the most eminent legal authority in England, argued that the Stamp Act was clearly within the power of Parliament, while Lord Camden, whose opinion was by no means to be despised, staked his reputation that the law was unconstitutional. Mr. Grenville, in his precise way, laid it down as axiomatic that since "Great Britain protects America, America is therefore bound to yield obedience"; if not, he desired to know when Americans were emancipated. Whereupon Mr. Pitt, springing up, desired to know when they were made slaves. The Great Commoner rejoiced that America had resisted, and expressed the belief that three millions of people so dead to all the feelings of liberty as voluntarily to submit to be made slaves would be very fit instruments to make slaves of all Englishmen.

Honorable members were more disposed to listen to Mr. Pitt than to vote with him; and were doubtless less influenced by his hot eloquence than by the representations of English merchants to the effect that trade was being ruined by Mr. Grenville's measures. Sir George Seville, honorable member for Yorkshire, spoke the practical mind of business men when he wrote to Lord Rockingham: "Our trade is hurt; what the devil have you been doing? For our part, we don't pretend to understand your politics and American matters, but our trade is hurt: pray remedy it, and a plague of you if you won't." This was not so eloquent as Mr. Pitt's speech, but still very eloquent in its way and more easily followed than Mr. Pitt's theory that "taxation is no part of the governing or legislative power."

Constitutional arguments, evenly balanced pro and con, were not certain to change many minds, while such brief statements as that of Sir George Seville, although clearly revealing the opinion of that gentleman, did little to enlighten the House on the merits of the question. That members might have every opportunity to inform themselves about America, the ministers thought it worth while to have Benjamin Franklin of Philadelphia, printer and Friend of the Human

Race, brought before the bar of the House to make such statements of fact or opinion as might be desired of him. The examination was a long one; the questions very much to the point; the replies very ready and often more to the point than the questions. With much exact information the provincial printer maintained that the colonists, having taxed themselves heavily in support of the last war, were not well able to pay more taxes, and that, even if they were abundantly able, the sugar duties and the stamp tax were improper measures. The stamps, in remote districts, would frequently require more in postage to obtain than the value of the tax. The sugar duties had already greatly diminished the volume of colonial trade, while both the duties and the tax, having to be paid in silver, were draining America of its specie and thus making it impossible for merchants to import from England to the same extent as formerly. It was well known that at the moment Americans were indebted to English merchants to the amount of several million pounds sterling, which they were indeed willing, as English merchants themselves said, but unable to pay. Necessarily, therefore, Americans were beginning to manufacture their own cloth, which they could very well do. Before their old clothes were worn out they "would have new ones of their own making."

Against the Stamp Act, honorable members were reminded, there was a special objection to be urged. It was thought with good reason to be unconstitutional, which would make its application difficult, if not impossible. Troops might no doubt be sent to enforce it, but troops would find no enemy to contend with, no men in arms; they would find no rebellion in America, although they might indeed create one. Pressed by Mr. Townshend to say whether the colonies might not, on the ground of Magna Carta, as well deny the validity of external as internal taxes, the Doctor was not ready to commit himself on that point. It was true many arguments had lately been used in England to show Americans that, if Parliament has no right to tax them internally, it has none to tax them externally, or to make any other law to bind them; in reply to which, he could only say that "at present they do not reason so, but in time they may possibly be convinced by these arguments."

Whether the Parliament was truly enlightened and resolved by statistical information and lofty

constitutional argument is not certainly known;
but it is known that the King, whose steady mind
did not readily change, was still opposed to the
repeal, a fact supposed to be not without influence in unsettling the opinions of some honorable
members.   Lord Mansfield had discreetly advised
His Majesty that although it was contrary to the
spirit of the constitution to "endeavour by His
Majesty's name to carry questions in Parliament,
yet where the lawful rights of the King and Parliament were to be asserted and maintained, he
thought the making His Majesty's opinion in
support of those rights to be known, was very fit
and becoming."

The distinction was subtle, but perhaps not
too subtle for a great lawyer. It was apparently
not too subtle for a Patriot King, since certain
noble lords who could be counted on to know the
King's wishes conveyed information to the proper
persons that those who found it against their
conscience to vote for the repeal would not for
that reason be received coldly at St. James's
Palace. In order to preserve the constitution as
well as to settle the question of the repeal on its
merits, Lord Rockingham and the Earl of Shelburne obtained an interview with the King at

which they pointed out to him the manifest irregularity of such a procedure, and in addition expressed their conviction that, on account of the high excitement in the City, failure to repeal the Stamp Act would be attended with very serious consequences.   Whether to preserve the Constitution, or to allow the repeal to be determined on its merits, or for some other reason, the King at last gave in writing his consent to the ministers' measure.   On February 22, by a vote of 275 to 167, Mr. Conway was given leave to bring in the bill for a total repeal of the Stamp Act.   The bill was accordingly brought in, passed by both houses, and on March 18 assented to by the King.

In the colonies the repeal was thought to be a victory for true principles of government, at least a tacit admission by the mother country that the American interpretation of the Constitution was the correct one.   No Englishman denied that the repeal was an American victory; and there were some, like Pitt and Camden, who preferred the constitutional theories of Daniel Dulaney[1] to those of George Grenville.   But most Englishmen

[1] Daniel Dulaney, of Maryland, was the author of a pamphlet entitled *Considerations on the Propriety of Imposing Taxes on the British Colonies.*   Pitt, in his speech on the repeal of the Stamp Act, referred to this pamphlet as a masterly performance.

who took the trouble to have any views on such recondite matters, having in general a poor opinion of provincial logic, easily dismissed the whole matter with the convincing phrase of Charles Townshend that the distinction between internal and external taxes was "perfect nonsense." The average Briton, taking it for granted that all the subtle legal aspects of the question had been thoroughly gone into by Lord Mansfield, was content to read Mr. Soame Jenyns, a writer of verse and member of the Board of Trade, who in a leisure hour had recently turned his versatile mind to the consideration of colonial rights with the happiest results. In twenty-three very small pages he had disposed of the "Objections to the Taxation of Our American Colonies" in a manner highly satisfactory to himself and doubtless also to the average reading Briton, who understood constitutional questions best when they were "briefly considered," and when they were humorously expounded in pamphlets that could be had for sixpence.

Having a logical mind, Mr. Jenyns easily perceived that taxes could be objected to on two grounds: the ground of right and the ground of expediency. In his opinion the right of Parliament to lay taxes on America and the expediency of doing so at the present moment were propositions so clear that any man, in order not to bring his intelligence in question, needed to apologize for undertaking to defend them. Mr. Jenyns wished it known that he was not the man to carry owls to Athens, and that he would never have thought it necessary to prove either the right or the expediency of taxing our American colonies, "had not many arguments been lately flung out . . . which with insolence equal to their absurdity deny them both." With this conciliatory preliminary disclaimer of any lack of intelligence on his own part, Mr. Jenyns proceeded to point out, in his most happy vein, how unsubstantial American reasoning really appeared when, brushing aside befogging irrelevancies, you once got to the heart of the question.

The heart of the question was the proposition that there should be no taxation without representation; upon which principle it was necessary to observe only that many individuals in England, such as copyholders and leaseholders, and many communities, such as Manchester and Birmingham, were taxed in Parliament without being represented there. If Americans quoted you "Lock, Sidney,

Selden, and many other great names to prove that every Englishman . . . is still represented in Parliament," he would only ask why, since Englishmen are all represented in Parliament, are not all Americans represented in exactly the same way? Either Manchester is not represented or Massachusetts is. "Are Americans not British subjects? Are they not Englishmen? Or are they only Englishmen when they solicit protection, but not Englishmen when taxes are required to enable this country to protect them?" Americans said they had Assemblies of their own to tax them, which was a privilege granted them by charter, without which "that liberty which every Englishman has a right to is torn from them, they are all slaves, and all is lost." Colonial charters were, however, "undoubtedly no more than those of all corporations, which empower them to make bye-laws." As for "liberty," the word had so many meanings,"having within a few years been used as a synonymous term for Blasphemy, Bawdy, Treason, Libels, Strong Beer, and Cyder," that Mr. Jenyns could not presume to say what it meant.

Against the expediency of the taxes, Mr. Jenyns found that two objections had been raised: that the time was improper and the manner wrong.

As to the manner, the colonies themselves had in a way prescribed it, since they had not been able at the request of ministers to suggest any other. The time Mr. Jenyns thought most propitious, a point upon which he grew warm and almost serious.

Can any time be more proper to require some assistance from our colonies, to preserve to themselves their present safety, than when this country is almost undone by procuring it?   Can any time be more proper to impose some tax upon their trade, than when they are enabled to rival us in their manufactures by the encouragement and protection which we have given them?   Can any time be more proper to oblige them to settle handsome incomes on their governors, than when we find them unable to procure a subsistence on any other terms than those of breaking all their instructions, and betraying the rights of their Sovereign? . . . Can there be a more proper time to force them to maintain an army at their expence, than when that army is necessary for their own protection, and we are utterly unable to support it?   Lastly, can there be a more proper time for this mother country to leave off feeding out of her own vitals these children whom she has nursed up, than when they are arrived at such strength and maturity as to be well able to provide for themselves, and ought rather with filial duty to give some assistance to her distresses?

Americans, after all, were not the only ones who might claim to have a grievance!

It was upon a lighter note, not to end in anti-climax, that Mr. Jenyns concluded his able pamphlet. He had heard it hinted that allowing the colonies representation in Parliament would be a simple plan for making taxes legal. The impracticability of this plan, he would not go into, since the plan itself had nowhere been seriously pressed, but he would, upon that head, offer the following consideration:

I have lately seen so many specimens of the great powers of speech of which these American gentlemen are possessed, that I should be much afraid that the sudden importation of so much eloquence at once would greatly endanger the safety of the government of this country. . . . If we can avail ourselves of these taxes on no other condition, I shall never look upon it as a measure of frugality, being perfectly satisfied that in the end, it will be much cheaper for us to pay their army than their orators.

Mr. Jenyns's pamphlet, which could be had for sixpence, was widely read, with much appreciation for its capital wit and extraordinary common sense; more widely read in England than Mr. James Otis's *Rights of the British Colonies Asserted and Proved* or Daniel Dulaney's *Considerations on the Propriety of Imposing Taxes on the British Colo-*

nies; and it therefore did much more than these able pamphlets to clarify English opinion on the rights of Parliament and the expediency of taxing America. No one could deny that Government had yielded in the face of noisy clamor and forcible resistance. To yield under the circumstances may have been wise or not; but Government had not yielded on any ground of right, but had on the contrary most expressly affirmed, in the Declaratory Act, that "the King's Majesty, by and with the advice of the lords spiritual and temporal, and commons of Great Britain, in Parliament assembled, had, hath, and of right ought to have, full power and authority to make such laws and statutes of sufficient force and validity to bind the colonies and people of America, subjects of the Crown of Great Britain, in all cases whatsoever." Government had not even denied the expediency of taxing America, the total repeal of the Stamp Act and the modification of the Sugar Act having been carried on a consideration of the inexpediency of these particular taxes only. Taxes not open to the same objection might in future be found, and doubtless must be found, inasmuch as the troops were still retained in America and the Quartering Act continued in force there. For new taxes, however, it would doubtless be necessary to await the formation of a new ministry.

The formation of a new ministry was not an unusual occurrence in the early years of King George the Third. No one supposed that Lord Rockingham could hold on many months; and as early as July, 1766, all London knew that Mr. Pitt had been sent for. The coming and going of great men in times of ministerial crisis was always a matter of interest; but the formation of that ministry of all the factions which the Patriot King had long desired was something out of the ordinary, the point of greatest speculation being how many irreconcilables Mr. Pitt (the Earl of Chatham he was now) could manage to get seated about a single table. From the point of view of irreconcilability, no one was more eligible than Mr. Charles Townshend, at that moment Paymaster of the Forces, a kind of *enfant terrible* of English politics, of whom Horace Walpole could say, with every likelihood of being believed, that "his speech of last Friday, made while half drunk, was all wit and indiscretion; nobody but he could have made it, nobody but he would have made it if he could. He beat Lord Chatham in language, Burke in metaphors, Grenville in presumption, Rigby in impudence, himself in folly, and everybody in good humour."

This gentleman, much to his astonishment, one day received the following note from Lord Chatham: "Sir: You are too great a magnitude not to be in a responsible place; I intend to propose you for Chancellor of the Exchequer, and must desire to have your answer by nine o'clock tonight."   Mr. Townshend was dismayed as well as astonished, his dismay arising from the fact that the office of Chancellor of the Exchequer was worth but £2700, which was precisely £4300 less than he was then receiving as Paymaster of the Forces.   To be a great magnitude on small pay had its disadvantages, and Mr. Townshend, after remaining home all day in great distress of mind, begged Mr. Pitt to be allowed to retain the office of Paymaster; which was no sooner granted than he changed his mind and begged Mr. Pitt to be allowed to accept the Exchequer place, which Mr. Pitt at first refused and was only persuaded to grant finally upon the intercession of the Duke of Grafton.   The day following, Mr. Townshend accordingly informed the King that he had decided, in view of the urgent representations of the Earl

of Chatham, to accept the office of Chancellor of
the Exchequer in his Majesty's new ministry.

No one supposed, least of all himself, that this
delightful man would have any influence in formulating the policies of the Chatham ministry.
Lord Chatham's policies were likely to be his own;
and in the present case, so far as America was
concerned, they were not such as could be readily
associated with Mr. Townshend's views, so far as
those views were known or were not inconsistent.
For dealing with America, the Earl of Shelburne,
because of his sympathetic understanding of colonial matters, had been brought into the ministry to formulate a comprehensive and conciliatory plan; as for the revenue, always the least
part of Lord Chatham's difficulties as it was the
chief of Mr. Grenville's, it was thought that the
possessions of the East India Company, if taken
over by the Government, would bring into the
Treasury sums quite sufficient to pay the debt
as well as to relieve the people, in England and
America at least, of those heavy taxes which Mr.
Grenville and his party had thought necessarily
involved in the extension of empire. It was a
curious chapter of accidents that brought all
these well-laid plans to nought. Scarcely was the

ministry formed when the Earl of Chatham, inca-
pacitated by the gout, retired into a seclusion that
soon became impenetrable; and "even before this
resplendent orb was entirely set, and while the
western horizon was in a blaze with his descending glory, on the opposite quarter of the heavens
arose another luminary, and, for his hour, became
lord of the ascendant." This luminary was Mr.
Charles Townshend.

Mr. Townshend was the "delight and ornament"
of the House, as Edmund Burke said. Never was
a man in any country of "more pointed and
finished wit, or (where his passions were not concerned) of a more refined, exquisite, and pene-
trating judgment"; never a man to excel him
in "luminous explanation and display of his subject," nor ever one less tedious or better able to
conform himself exactly to the temper of the House
which he seemed to guide because he was always
sure to follow it. In 1765 Mr. Townshend had
voted for the Stamp Act, but in 1766, when the
Stamp Act began to be no favorite, he voted for
the repeal, and would have spoken for it too, if
an illness had not prevented him. And now, in
1767, Mr. Townshend was Chancellor of the Exchequer, and as such responsible for the revenue; a

man without any of that temperamental obstinacy which persists in opinions once formed, and without any fixed opinions to persist in; but quite disposed, according to habit, to "hit the House just between wind and water," and to win its applause by speaking for the majority, or by "haranguing inimitably on both sides" when the majority was somewhat uncertain.

In January, 1767, when Lord Chatham was absent and the majority was very uncertain, Mr. Grenville took occasion, in the debate upon the extraordinaries for the army in England and America, to move that America, like Ireland. should support its own establishment. The opportunity was one which Mr. Townshend could not let pass. Much to the astonishment of every one and most of all to that of his colleagues in the ministry, he supported Mr. Grenville's resolution, declaring himself now in favor of the Stamp Act which he had voted to repeal, treating "Lord Chatham's distinction between internal and external taxation as contemptuously as Mr. Grenville had done," and pledging himself able, if necessary, to find a revenue in America nearly adequate to the proposed project. The Earl of Shelburne, in great distress of mind, at once wrote to Lord

Chatham, relating the strange if characteristic
conduct of the Chancellor of the Exchequer, and
declaring himself entirely ignorant of the intentions
of his colleagues. It was indeed an anomalous
situation. If Lord Chatham's policies were still
to be considered those of the ministry, Mr. Townshend might be said to be in opposition, a circumstance which made "many people think Lord
Chatham ill at St. James's" only.

Lord Chatham was not ill at St. James's. He
was most likely very well at St. James's, being
unable to appear there, thus leaving the divided
ministry amenable to the King's management or
helpless before a factious Opposition. The opportunity of the Opposition came when the Chancellor of the Exchequer, in February, proposed to
continue the land tax at four shillings for one year
more, after which time, he thought, it might be
reduced to three shillings in view of additional
revenues to be obtained from the East India Company. But Opposition saw no reason why, in
view of the revenue which Mr. Townshend had
pledged himself to find in America, a shilling
might not be taken from the land at once, a proposal which Mr. Dowdeswell moved should be
done, and which was accordingly voted through

the influence of Mr. Grenville and the Duke of
Bedford, who had formerly carried the Stamp
Act, aided by the Rockingham Whigs who had
formerly repealed it.   If Lord Chatham was ill at
St. James's, this was a proper time to resign.   It
was doubtless a proper time to resign in any case.
But Lord Chatham did not resign.   In March he
came to London, endeavored to replace Mr. Townshend by Lord North, which he failed to do, and
then retired to Bath to be seen no more, leaving
Mr. Townshend more than ever "master of the
revels."

Mr. Townshend did not resign either, but continued in office, quite undisturbed by the fact that
a cardinal measure of the ministry had been de-
cisively voted down.   Mr. Townshend reasoned
that if Opposition would not support the ministry,
all difficulties would be straightened out by the
ministry's supporting the Opposition.   This was
the more reasonable since Opposition had perhaps
been right after all, so far as the colonies were
concerned.   Late reports from that quarter seemed
to indicate that the repeal of the Stamp Act, far
from satisfying the Americans, had only confirmed
that umbrageous people in a spirit of licentiousness, which was precisely what Opposition had

predicted as the sure result of any weak concession.   The New York Assembly, it now appeared,
refused to make provision for the troops according
to the terms of the Quartering Act; New York
merchants were petitioning for a further modification of the trade acts; the precious Bostonians,
wrangling refined doctrinaire points with Governor Bernard, were making interminable difficulties
about compensating the sufferers from the Stamp
Act riots.   If Lord Chatham, in February, 1767,
could go so far as to say that the colonies had
"drunk deep of the baneful cup of infatuation,"
Mr. Townshend, having voted for the Stamp Act
and for its repeal, might well think, in May, that
the time was ripe for a return to rigorous measures.

On May 13, in a speech which charmed the
House, Mr. Townshend opened his plan for settling
the colonial question.   The growing spirit of insub-
ordination, which must be patent to all, he thought
could be most effectively checked by making an
example of New York, where defiance was at
present most open; for which purpose it was proposed that the meetings of the Assembly of that
province be totally suspended until it should have
complied with the terms of the Mutiny Act.   As
one chief source of power in colonial assemblies

which contributed greatly to make them insubordi-
nate was the dependence of executive officials upon
them for salaries, Mr. Townshend now renewed
the proposal, which he had formerly brought forward in 1763, to create an independent civil list
for the payment of governors and judges from
England.   The revenue for such a civil list would
naturally be raised in America.   Mr. Townshend
would not, however, venture to renew the Stamp
Act, which had been so opposed on the ground
of its being an internal tax.   He was free to say
that the distinction between internal and external
taxes was perfect nonsense; but, since the logical
Americans thought otherwise, he would concede
the point and would accordingly humor them by
laying only external duties, which he thought
might well be on various kinds of glass and paper,
on red and white lead, and upon teas, the duties
to be collected in colonial ports upon the importation of these commodities from England.
It was estimated that the duties might altogether
make about £40,000, if the collection were properly attended to; and in order that the collection
might be properly attended to, and for the more
efficient administration of the American customs
in general, Mr. Townshend further recommended

that a Board of Customs Commissioners be created and established in Massachusetts Bay. With slight opposition, all these recommendations were enacted into law; and the Commissioners of the Customs, shortly afterward appointed by the King, arrived in Boston in November, 1767.

At Boston, the Commissioners found much to be done in the way of collecting the customs, particularly in the matter of Madeira wines. Madeira wines were much drunk in the old Bay colony, being commonly imported directly from the islands, without too much attention to the duty of £7 per ton lawfully required in that case. Mr. John Hancock, a popular Boston merchant, did a thriving business in this way; and his sloop *Liberty*, in the ordinary course of trade, carrying six pipes of "good saleable Madeira" for the coffee-house retailers, four pipes of the "very best" for his own table, and "two pipes more of the best . . . for the Treasurer of the province," entered the harbor on May 9, 1768. In the evening Mr. Thomas Kirk, tide-waiter, acting for the Commissioners, boarded the sloop, where he found the captain, Nat Bernard, and also, by some chance, another of Mr. Hancock's skippers, young James Marshall, together with half a dozen of his friends. They sat

with punch served by the captain all round until
nine o'clock, when young James Marshall casually
asked if a few casks might not as well be set on
shore that evening.   Mr. Kirk replied that it could
not be done with his leave; whereupon he found
himself "hoved down" into the cabin and confined
there for three hours, from which point of disadvantage he could distinctly hear overhead "a
noise of many people at work, a-hoisting out of
goods."   In due time Mr. Kirk was released, having suffered no injury, except perhaps a little in
his official character.   Next day Mr. Hancock's
cargo was duly entered, no pipes of Madeira
listed: and to all appearance the only serious aspect of the affair was that young James Marshall
died before morning, it was thought from over-
exertion and excitement.

Very likely few people in Boston knew anything
about this interesting episode; and a month later
much excitement was accordingly raised by the
news that Mr. Hancock's sloop *Liberty* had been
ordered seized for non-payment of customs.   A
crowd watched the ship towed, for safe-keeping,
under the guns of the *Romney* in the harbor.
When the Commissioners, who had come down
to see the thing done, left the wharf they were

roughly handled by the incensed people; and in
the evening windows of some of their houses were
broken, and a boat belonging to a collector was
hauled on shore and burnt on the Common.
Governor Bernard at last informed the Commissioners that he could not protect them in
Boston, whereupon they retired with their families to the *Romney*, and later to Castle William.
There they continued, under difficulties, the work
of systematizing the American customs; and not
without success, inasmuch as the income from the
duties during the years from 1768 to 1774 averaged
about £30,000 sterling, at an annual cost to the
revenue of not more than £13,000. This saving
was nevertheless not effected without the establishment at Boston, on the recommendation of
the Commissioners, of two regiments of the line
which arrived September 28, 1768, and were
landed under the guns of eight men-of-war, without opposition. The cost of maintaining the two
regiments in Boston was doubtless not included
in the £13,000 charged to the revenue as the
annual expense of collecting £30,000 of customs.

In spite of the two regiments of the line, with
artillery, Boston was not quiet in this year 1768.
The soldiers acted decently enough, no doubt; but

their manners were very British and their coats were red, and "their simple presence," conveying every day the suggestion of compulsion, was "an intolerable grievance." Every small matter was magnified. The people, says Hutchinson, "had been used to answer to the call of the town watch in the night, yet they did not like to answer to the frequent calls of the centinels posted at the barracks; . . . and either a refusal to answer, or an answer accompanied with irritating language, endangered the peace of the town." On Sundays, especially, the Boston mind found something irreverent, something at the very least irrelevant, in the presence of the bright colored and highly secular coats; while the noise of fife and drum, so disturbing to the sabbath calm, called forth from the Selectmen a respectful petition to the general requesting him to "dispense with the band."

These were but slight matters; but as time passed little grievances accumulated on both sides until the relation between the people and the soldiers was one of settled hostility, and at last, after two years, the tense situation culminated in the famous Boston Massacre. On the evening of March 5, 1770, there was an alarm of fire, false as it turned out, which brought many people into the streets,

especially boys, whom one may easily imagine
catching up, as they ran, handfuls of damp snow
to make snowballs. For snowballs, there could be
no better target than red-coated sentinels standing erect and motionless at the post of duty; and
it chanced that one of these individuals, stationed before the Customs House door, was pelted
with the close-packed missiles. Being several
times struck, he called for aid, the guard turned
out, and a crowd gathered. One of the soldiers
was presently knocked down, another was hit by a
club, and at last six or seven shots were fired, with
or without orders, the result of which was four
citizens lying dead on the snow-covered streets of
Boston.

The Boston Massacre was not as serious as the
Massacre of Saint Bartholomew or the Sicilian
Vespers; but it served to raise passion to a white
heat in the little provincial town. On the next
day there was assembled, under the skillful leadership of Samuel Adams, a great town meeting which
demanded in no uncertain terms the removal of the
troops from Boston. Under the circumstances,
six hundred British soldiers would have fared badly
in Boston; and in order to prevent further blood-
shed, acting Governor Hutchinson finally gave the

order. Within a fortnight, the two small regiments retired to Castle William. Seven months later Captain Preston and other soldiers implicated in the riot were tried before a Boston jury. Ably defended by John Adams and Josiah Quincy, they were all acquitted on the evidence, except two who were convicted and lightly punished for manslaughter.

As it happened, the Boston Massacre occurred on the 5th of March, 1770, which was the very day that Lord North rose in the House of Commons to propose the partial repeal of the Townshend duties. This outcome was not unconnected with events that had occurred in America during the eighteen months since the landing of the troops in Boston in September, 1768. In 1768, John Adams could not have foretold the Boston Massacre, or have foreseen that he would himself incur popular displeasure for having defended the soldiers. But he could, even at that early date, divine the motives of the British government in sending the troops to Boston. To his mind, "the very appearance of the troops in Boston was a strong proof . . . that the determination of Great Britain to subjugate us was too deep and inveterate to be altered." All the measures of ministry seemed indeed to confirm that view. Mr. Townshend's condescension in accepting the colonial distinction between internal and external taxes was clearly only a subtle maneuver designed to conceal an attack upon liberty far more dangerous than the former attempts of Mr. Grenville. After all, Mr. Townshend was probably right in thinking the distinction of no importance, the main point being whether, as Lord Chatham had said, the Parliament could by any kind of taxes "take money out of their pockets without their consent."

Duties on glass and tea certainly would take money out of their pockets without their consent, and therefore it must be true that taxes could be rightly laid only by colonial assemblies, in which alone Americans could be represented. But of what value was it to preserve the abstract right of taxation by colonial assemblies if meanwhile the assemblies themselves might, by act of Parliament, be abolished? And had not the New York Assembly been suspended by act of Parliament? And were not the new duties to be used to pay governors and judges, thus by subtle indirection undermining the very basis of legislative independence? And now, in the year 1768, the Massachusetts Assembly, having sent a circular letter to the other colonies requesting concerted action in defense of their liberties, was directed by Lord Hillsborough, speaking in his Majesty's name, "to rescind the resolution which gave birth to the circular letter from the Speaker, and to declare their disapprobation of, and dissent to, that rash and hasty proceeding." Clearly, it was no mere question of taxation but the larger question of legislative independence that now confronted Americans.

A more skillful dialectic was required to defend American rights against the Townshend duties than against the Stamp Act. It was a somewhat stubborn fact that Parliament had for more than a hundred years passed laws effectively regulating colonial trade, and for regulating trade had imposed duties, some of which had brought into the Exchequer a certain revenue. Americans, wishing to be thought logical as well as loyal, could not well say at this late date that Parliament had no right to lay duties in regulation of trade. Must they then submit to the Townshend duties? Or was it possible to draw a line, making a distinction, rather more subtle than the old one between internal and external taxes, between duties for regulation and duties for revenue? This latter feat was undertaken by Mr. John

Dickinson of Pennsylvania, anonymously, under the guise of a simple but intelligent and virtuous farmer whose arcadian existence had confirmed in him an instinctive love of liberty and had supplied him with the leisure to meditate at large upon human welfare and the excellent British Constitution.

Mr. Dickinson readily granted America to be dependent upon Great Britain, "as much dependent upon Great Britain as one perfectly free people can be on another." But it appeared axiomatic to the unsophisticated mind of a simple farmer that no people could be free if taxed without its consent, and that Parliament had accordingly no right to lay any taxes upon the colonies; from which it followed that the sole question in respect to duties laid on trade was whether they were intended for revenue or for regulation. Intention in such matters was of primary importance, since all duties were likely to be regulative to some extent. It might be objected that "it will be difficult for any persons but the makers of the laws to determine which of them are made for regulation of trade, and which for raising a revenue." This was true enough but at present of academic importance only, inasmuch as the makers of the Sugar

Act, the Stamp Act, and the Townshend duties had conveniently and very clearly proclaimed their intention to be the raising of a revenue. Yet this question, academic now, might soon become extremely practical. The makers of laws might not always express their intention so explicitly; they might, with intention to raise a revenue, pass acts professing to be for regulation only; and therefore, since "names will not change the nature of things," Americans ought "firmly to believe . . . that unless the most watchful attention be exerted, a new servitude may be slipped upon us under the sanction of usual and respectable terms." In such case the intention should be inferred from the nature of the act; and the Farmer, for his part, sincerely hoped that his countrymen "would never, to their latest existence, want understanding sufficient to discover the intentions of those who rule over them."

Mr. Dickinson's *Farmer's Letters* were widely read and highly commended. The argument, subtle but clear, deriving the nature of an act from the intention of its makers, and the intention of its makers from the nature of the act, contributed more than any other exposition to convince Americans that they "have the same right that all states have, of judging when their privileges are invaded."

"As much dependent on Great Britain as one perfectly free people can be on another," the Farmer said. Englishmen might be excused for desiring a more precise delimitation of parliamentary jurisdiction than could be found in this phrase, as well as for asking what clear legal ground there was for making any delimitation at all. To the first point, Mr. Dickinson said in effect that Parliament had not the right to tax the colonies and that it had not the right to abolish their assemblies through which they alone could tax themselves. The second point Mr Dickinson did not clearly answer, although it was undoubtedly most fundamental. To this point Mr. Samuel Adams had given much thought; and in letters which he drafted for the Massachusetts Assembly, in the famous circular letter particularly, and in the letter of January 12, 1769, sent to the Assembly's agent in England, Mr. Dennys De Berdt, Mr. Adams formulated a theory designed to show that the colonies were "subordinate" but not subject to the British Parliament. The delimitation of colonial and parliamentary jurisdictions Mr. Adams achieved by subordinating all legis-

lative authority to an authority higher than any
positive law, an authority deriving its sanction
from the fixed and universal law of nature.   This
higher authority, which no legislature could "overleap without destroying its own foundation," was
the British Constitution.

Mr. Adams spoke of the British Constitution
with immense confidence, as something singularly
definite and well known, the provisions of which
were clearly ascertainable; which singular effect
doubtless came from the fact that he thought
of it, not indeed as something written down on
paper and deposited in archives of state, but as a
series of propositions which, as they were saying
in France, were indelibly "written in the hearts of
all men."   The British Constitution, he said, like
the constitution of every free state, "is fixed,"
having its foundation not in positive law, which
would indeed give Parliament an ultimate and
therefore a despotic authority, but in "the law of
God and nature."   There were in the British
Empire many legislatures, all deriving their
authority from, and all finding their limitations
in, the Constitution.   Parliament had certainly
a supreme or superintending legislative authority
in the Empire, as the colonial assemblies had a

"subordinate," in the sense of a local, legislative authority; but neither the Parliament nor any colonial assembly could "overleap the Constitution without destroying its own foundation." And therefore, since the Constitution is founded "in the law of God and nature," and since "it is an essential natural right that a man shall quietly enjoy and have the sole disposal of his property," the Americans must enjoy this right equally with Englishmen, and Parliament must be bound to respect this right in the colonies as well as in England; from which it followed irresistibly that the consent of the colonies to any taxation must be sought exclusively in their own assemblies, it being manifestly impossible for that consent to be "constitutionally had in Parliament."

It was commonly thought in America that Mr. Adams, although not a judge, had a singular gift for constitutional interpretation. Far-sighted men could nevertheless believe that a powerful party in England, inspired by inveterate hatred of America and irretrievably bent upon her ruin, would pronounce all his careful distinctions ridiculous and would still reply to every argument by the mere assertion, as a fact behind which one could not go, that Parliament had always had and

must therefore still have full power to bind the
colonies in all cases whatsoever.   If Britain would
not budge from this position, Americans would
soon be confronted with the alternative of admit-
ting Parliament to have full power or denying it
to have any.

With that sharp-set alternative in prospect, it
would be well to keep in mind the fact that arguments lost carrying power in proportion to their
subtlety; and in the opinion of so good a judge as
Benjamin Franklin the reasoning of Mr. Adams
and Mr. Dickinson was perhaps not free from this
grave disadvantage.

I am not yet master [he was free to confess] of the
idea these . . . writers have of the relation between
Britain and her colonies.   I know not what the Boston
people mean by the "subordination" they acknowledge
in their Assembly to Parliament, while they deny its
power to make laws for them, nor what bounds the
Farmer sets to the power he acknowledges in Parliament to "regulate the trade of the colonies," it being
difficult to draw lines between duties for regulation
and those for revenue; and, if the Parliament is to be
the judge, it seems to me that establishing such a
principle of distinction will amount to little.   The
more I have thought and read on the subject, the more
I find myself confirmed in opinion, that no middle
ground can be well maintained, I mean not clearly with

intelligible arguments. Something might be made of either of the extremes: that Parliament has a power to make *all laws* for us, or that it has a power to make *no laws* for us; and I think the arguments for the latter more numerous and weighty, than those for the former.

The good Doctor had apparently read and thought a great deal about the matter since the day when Mr. Grenville had called him in to learn if there were good objections to be urged against the Stamp Act.

Practical men were meanwhile willing to allow the argument to take whatever direction the exigencies of the situation might require, being ready to believe that Mr. Dickinson counseled well and that Mr. Franklin counseled well; being nevertheless firmly convinced from past experience that an Englishman's ability to see reason was never great except when his pocket was touched. Practical men were therefore generally of the opinion that they could best demonstrate their rights by exhibiting their power. This happily, they could do by bringing pressure to bear upon English merchants by taking money out of *their* pockets — without their consent to be sure but in a manner strictly legal — by means of non-importation agreements voluntarily entered into.

As early as October, 1767, the Boston merchants entered into such an agreement, which was however not very drastic and proved to be of no effect, as it was at first unsupported by the merchants in any other colony.   In April, 1768, the merchants of New York, seeing the necessity of concerted action, agreed not to import "any goods [save a very few enumerated articles] which shall be shipped from Great Britain after the first of October next; provided Boston and Philadelphia adopt similar measures by the first of June."   Philadelphia merchants said they were not opposed to the principle of non-importation, but greatly feared the New York plan would serve to create a monopoly by enabling men of means to lay in a large stock of goods before the agreement went into effect.   This was very true; but the objection, if it was an objection, proved not to be an insurmountable one.   Before the year was out, in the late summer for the most part, the merchants in all the commercial towns had subscribed to agreements, differing somewhat in detail, of which the substance was that they would neither import from Great Britain any commodities, nor buy or sell any which might inadvertently find their way in, until the duties imposed by the Townshend act should have been repealed.

The merchants' agreements were, for whatever reason, much better observed in some places than in others.   Imports from Great Britain to New York fell during the year 1769 from about £482,000 to about £74,000.   Imports into New England and into Pennsylvania declined a little more than one half; whereas in the southern colonies there was no decline at all, but on the contrary an increase, slight in the case of Maryland and Virginia and rather marked in the Carolinas.   In spite of these defections, the experiment was not without effect upon English merchants.   English merchants, but little interested in the decline or increase of trade to particular colonies, were chiefly aware that the total exportation to America was nearly a million pounds less in 1769 than in 1768.   Understanding little about colonial rights, but knowing only, as in 1766, that their "trade was hurt," they accordingly applied once more to Parliament for relief.   The commerce with America which was "so essential to afford employment and subsistence to the manufactures of these kingdoms, to augment the public revenue, to serve as a nursery for seamen, and to increase our navigation and maritime strength" —

this commerce, said the Merchants and Traders of the City of London Trading to America, "is at present in an alarming state of suspension"; and the Merchants and Traders of the City of London therefore humbly prayed Parliament to repeal the duties which were the occasion of their inconveniences.

The petition of the London merchants came before the House on March 5, 1770, that being the day fixed by Lord North for proposing, on behalf of the ministry, certain measures for America. No one, said the first minister, could be more free than himself to recognize the importance of American trade or more disposed to meet the wishes of the London merchants as far as possible. The inconveniences under which that trade now labored were manifest, but he could not think, with the petitioners, that these inconveniences arose from "the nature of the duties" so much as "through the medium of the dissatisfaction of the Americans, and those combinations and associations of which we have heard" — associations and combinations which had been called, in an address to the House, "unwarrantable," but which he for his part would go so far as to call illegal. These illegal combinations in America were obviously what caused the inconveniences of which the merchants complained. To the pressure of illegal combinations alone Parliament ought never to yield; and ministers wished it clearly understood that, if they were about to propose a repeal of some of the duties, they were not led to take this step from any consideration of the disturbances in the colonies.

On the contrary, the duties which it was now proposed to repeal — the duties on lead, glass, and paper — were to be repealed strictly on the ground that they ought never to have been laid, because duties on British manufactures were contrary to true commercial principles. Last year, when ministers had expressed, in a letter of Lord Hillsborough to the governors, their intention to repeal these duties, some members had been in favor of repealing all the duties and some were still in favor of doing so. As to that, the first minister could only say that he had not formerly been opposed to it and would not now be opposed to it, had the Americans, in response to the Earl of Hillsborough's letter, exhibited any disposition to cease their illegal disturbances or renounce their combinations. But the fact was that conditions in America had grown steadily worse since the Earl of Hillsborough's letter, and

never had been so bad as now; in view of which fact
ministers could not but think it wise to maintain
some tax as a matter of principle purely.   They
would therefore recommend that the tax on tea,
no burden certainly on anyone, be continued as a
concrete application of the right of Parliament to
tax the colonies.

In so far as they were designed to bring pressure
to bear upon the mother country, the merchants'
agreements were clearly not without a measure
of success, having helped perhaps to bring Parliament to the point of repealing the duties on lead,
glass, and paper, as well as to bring ministers to
the point of keeping the duty on tea.   Americans
generally were doubtless well pleased with this
effect; but not all Americans were able to regard
the experiment in non-importation with unquali-
fied approval in other respects.   Non-importation,
by diminishing the quantity and increasing the
price of commodities, involved a certain amount
of personal sacrifice.   This sacrifice, however, fell
chiefly on the consumers, the non-importation
not being under certain circumstances altogether
without advantage to merchants who faithfully
observed their pledges as well as to those who observed them only occasionally.   So long as their

warehouses, well stocked in advance, contained anything that could be sold at a higher price than formerly, non-importation was no bad thing even for those merchants who observed the agreement. For those who did not observe the agreement, as well as for those who engaged in the smuggling trade from Holland, it was no bad thing at any time, and it promised to become an increasingly excellent thing in exact proportion to the exhaustion of the fair trader's stock and the consequent advance in prices. As time passed, therefore, the fair trader became aware that the non-importation experiment, practically considered, was open to certain objections; whereas the unfair trader was more in favor of the experiment the longer it endured, being every day more convinced that the non-importation agreement ought to be continued and strictly adhered to as essential to the maintenance of American liberties.

The practical defects of non-importation were likely to be understood, by those who could ever understand them, in proportion to the decay of business; and in the spring of 1770 they were nowhere better understood than in New York, where the decay of business was most marked. This decrease was greatest in New York, so the mer-

chants maintained, because that city had been
most faithful in observing the agreement, importation having there fallen from £482,000 to
£74,000 during the year. It is possible, however,
that the decay of business in New York was due
in part and perhaps primarily to the retirement,
in November, 1768, of the last issues of the old
Bills of Credit, according to the terms of the Paper
Currency Act passed by Parliament during Mr.
Grenville's administration. As a result of this
retirement of all the paper money in the province,
money of any sort was exceedingly scarce during
the years 1769 and 1770. Lyon dollars were rarely
seen; and the quantity of Spanish silver brought
into the colony through the trade with the foreign
islands, formerly considerable but now greatly
diminished by the stricter enforcement of the
Townshend Trade Acts, was hardly sufficient for
local exchange alone, to say nothing of settling
heavy balances in London, although, fortunately
perhaps, there were in the year 1769 no heavy
London balances to be settled on account of the
faithful observance of the non-importation agreement by the merchants. The lack of money was
therefore doubtless a chief cause of the great
decay of business in New York; and some there

were who maintained that the faithful observance
of the non-importation agreement by the merchants was due to the decay of trade rather than
the decay of trade being due to the faithful observance of the non-importation agreement.

Whatever the true explanation of this academic
point might be, it was an undoubted fact that
business was more nearly at a standstill in New
York than elsewhere.   Accordingly, in the spring
of 1770, when money was rarely to be seen and
debtors were selling their property at one-half or
one-third of its former value in order to discharge
obligations long overdue, the fair trading merchants of New York were not disposed to continue
an experiment of which, as they said, they had
borne the chief burden to the advantage of others
and to their own impending ruin.   Zealous Sons of
Liberty, such as Alexander MacDougall and John
Lamb, popular leaders of the "Inhabitants" of the
city, were on the other hand determined that the
non-importation agreement should be maintained
unimpaired.   The hard times, they said, were due
chiefly to the monopoly prices exacted by the
wealthy merchants, who were not ruined at all,
who had on the contrary made a good thing out of
the non-importation as long as they had anything

to sell, and whose patriotism (God save the mark!) had now suddenly grown lukewarm only because they had disposed of all their goods, including "old moth-eaten clothes that had been rotting in the shops for years."

These aspersions the merchants knew how to ignore. Their determination not to continue the non-importation was nevertheless sufficiently indicated in connection with the annual celebration, in March, of the repeal of the Stamp Act. On this occasion the merchants refused to meet as formerly with the Sons of Liberty, but made provision for a dinner of their own at another place, where all the Friends of Liberty and Trade were invited to be present. Both dinners were well attended, and at both the repeal of the Stamp Act was celebrated with patriotic enthusiasm, the main difference being that whereas the Sons of Liberty drank a toast to Mr. MacDougall and to "a continuance of the non-importation agreement until the revenue acts are repealed," the Friends of Liberty and Trade ignored Mr. MacDougall and drank to "trade and navigation and a speedy removal of their embarrassments."

In the determination not to continue the old agreement, the Friends of Liberty and Trade were meanwhile strongly confirmed when it was learned that Britain was willing on her part to make concessions. By the middle of May it was known that the Townshend duties (except the duty on tea) had been repealed; and in June it was learned that Parliament had at last, after many representations from the Assembly, passed a special act permitting New York to issue £120,-000 in Bills of Credit receivable at the Treasury. It was thought that concession on the part of Great Britain ought in justice to meet with concession on the part of America. Accordingly, on the ground that other towns, and Boston in particular, were more active "in resolving what they ought to do than in doing what they had resolved," and on the ground that the present non-importation agreement no longer served "any other purpose than tying the hands of honest men, to let rogues, smugglers, and men of no character plunder their country," the New York merchants, on July 9, 1770, resolved that for the future they would import from Great Britain all kinds of commodities except such as might be subject to duties imposed by Parliament.

The New York merchants were on every hand loudly denounced for having betrayed the cause of liberty; but before the year was out the old agreement was everywhere set aside. Yet everywhere, as at New York, the merchants bound themselves not to import any British teas. The duty on British teas was slight. Americans might have paid the duty without increasing the price of their much prized luxury; ministers might have collected the same duty in England to the advantage of the Exchequer. That Britain should have insisted on this peppercorn in acknowledgement of her right, that America should have refused it in vindication of her liberty, may be taken as a high tribute from two eminently practical peoples to the power of abstract ideas.

CHAPTER V

A LITTLE DISCREET CONDUCT

It has been his [Thomas Hutchinson's] principle from a boy that mankind are to be governed by the discerning few, and it has been ever since his ambition to be the hero of the few. — *Samuel Adams.*

We have not been so quiet these five years. . . . If it were not for two or three Adamses, we should do well enough. — *Thomas Hutchinson.*

IN December, 1771, Horace Walpole, a persistent if not an infallible political prophet, was of opinion that all the storms that for a decade had distressed the Empire were at last happily blown over; among which storms he included, as relatively of minor importance, the disputes with the colonies. During two years following, this prediction might well have appeared to moderate minded men entirely justified. American affairs were barely mentioned in Parliament, and a few paragraphs in the *Annual Register* were thought sufficient to chronicle for English readers events of interest occurring across the Atlantic. In the colonies themselves an unwonted tranquillity prevailed. Rioting, as an established social custom, disappeared in most of the places where it had formerly been so much practised. The Sons of Liberty, retaining the semblance of an organization, were rarely in the public eye save at the annual celebrations of the repeal of the Stamp Act, quite harmless occasions devoted to the expression of patriotic sentiments. Merchants and landowners, again prosperous, were content to fall back into accustomed habits of life, conscious of duty done without too much stress, readily believing their liberties finally vindicated against encroachments from abroad and their privileges secure against unwarranted and dangerous pretensions at home. "The people appear to be weary of their altercations with the mother country," Mr. Johnson, the Connecticut agent, wrote to Wedderburn, in October, 1771; "a little discreet conduct on both sides would perfectly reëstablish that warm affection and respect towards Great Britain for which this country was once remarkable."

Discreet conduct was nowhere more necessary than in Massachusetts, where the people, perhaps

because they were much accustomed to them,
grew weary of altercations less easily than in most
colonies.   Yet even in Massachusetts there was
a marked waning of enthusiasm after the high
excitement occasioned by the Boston Massacre,
a certain disintegration of the patriot party.
James Otis recovered from a temporary fit of
insanity only to grow strangely suspicious of
Samuel Adams.   Mr. Hancock, discreetly holding
his peace, attended to his many thriving and very
profitable business ventures.   John Adams, somewhat unpopular for having defended and procured the acquittal of the soldiers implicated in
the Massacre, retired in high dudgeon from public
affairs to the practice of his profession; in high
dudgeon with everyone concerned — with himself
first of all, and with the people who so easily
forgot their interests and those who had served
them, and with the British Government and all
fawning tools of ministers, of whom Mr. Thomas
Hutchinson was chief.   Meanwhile, Mr. Hutchinson, so roughly handled in the secret diary of
the rising young lawyer, was the recipient of
new honors, having been made Governor of the
province to succeed Francis Bernard.   For once
finding himself almost popular, he thought he

perceived a disposition in all the colonies, and even in Massachusetts, to let the controversy subside. "Though there are a small majority sour enough, yet when they seek matter for protests, remonstrances, they are puzzled where to charge the grievances which they look for." The new Governor looked forward to happier days and an easy administration. "Hancock and most of the party are quiet," he said, "and all of them, except Adams, abate of their virulence. Adams would push the Continent into a rebellion tomorrow, if it was in his power."

No one, in the year 1770, was better fitted than Samuel Adams, either by talent and temperament or the circumstances of his position, to push the continent into a rebellion. Unlike most of his patriot friends, he had neither private business nor private profession to fall back upon when public affairs grew tame, his only business being, as one might say, the public business, his only profession the definition and defense of popular rights. In this profession, by dint of single-minded devotion to it through a course of years, he had indeed become wonderfully expert and had already achieved for himself the enviable position of known and named leader in every movement of opposition to royal or magisterial prerogative. In this connection no exploit had brought him so much distinction as his skillful management of the popular uprising which had recently forced Governor Hutchinson to withdraw the troops from Boston. The event was no by-play in the life of Samuel Adams, no amateur achievement accomplished on the side, but the serious business of a man who during ten years had abandoned all private pursuits and had embraced poverty to become a tribune of the people.

Samuel Adams had not inherited poverty nor had he, after all, exactly embraced it, but had as it were naturally drifted into it through indifference to worldly gain, the indifference which men of single and fixed purpose have for all irrelevant matters. The elder Samuel Adams was a merchant of substance and of such consequence in the town of Boston that in Harvard College, where students were named according to the prominence of their families, his son's name was fifth in a class of twenty-two. In 1748, upon the death of his father, Samuel Junior accordingly inherited a very decent property, considered so at least in that day — a spacious old house in Purchase Street together with a well-established malt business.

For business, however, the young man, and not so young either, was without any aptitude whatever, being entirely devoid of the acquisitive instinct and neither possessing nor ever being able to acquire any skill in the fine art of inducing people to give for things more than it cost to make them. These deficiencies the younger Adams had already exhibited before the death of his father, from whom he received on one occasion a thousand pounds, half of which he promptly loaned to an impecunious friend, and which he would in any case doubtless have lost, as he soon did the other half, on his own account. In such incompetent hands the malt business soon fell to be a liability rather than an asset. Other liabilities accumulated, notably one incurred by the tax collectors of the town of Boston, of whom Samuel Adams was one during the years from 1756 to 1764. For one reason or another, on Adams's part certainly on account of his humane feelings and general business inefficiency, the collectors fell every year a little behind in the collections, and one day found themselves declared on the official records to be indebted to the town in the sum of £9,878. This indebtedness Mr. Hutchinson and other gentlemen not well disposed towards Samuel Adams conveniently and frequently referred to in later years as a "defalcation."

In this year of 1764, when he had lost his entire patrimony except the old house in Purchase Street, now somewhat rusty for want of repair, Samuel Adams was married to Elizabeth Wells. It was his second marriage, the first having taken place in 1749, of which the fruit was a son and a daughter. Samuel Adams was then — it was the year of the Sugar Act — forty-two years old; that is to say, at the age when a man's hair begins to turn gray, when his character is fixed, when his powers, such as they are, are fully matured; well known as a "poor provider," an improvident man who had lost a fair estate, had failed in business, and was barely able, and sometimes not able, to support his small family. These mundane matters concerned Samuel Adams but little. To John Adams he said on one occasion that "he never looked forward in life; never planned, laid a scheme, or formed a design for laying up anything for himself or others after him." This was the truth, inexplicable as it must have seemed to his more provident cousin. It was even less than the truth: during the years following 1764, Samuel Adams renounced all pretense of private business, giving himself wholly to public affairs, while his good wife, with excellent management, made his stipend as clerk of the Assembly serve for food, and obtained, through the generosity of friends or her own ingenious labors, indispensable clothes for the family. Frugality, that much lauded virtue in the eighteenth century, needed not to be preached in the old Purchase Street home; but life went on there, somehow or other, decently enough, not without geniality yet with evident piety. The old Bible is still preserved from which each evening some member of the family read a chapter, and at every meal the head of the house said grace, returning thanks for God's benefits.

If Samuel Adams at the age of forty-two was known for a man who could not successfully manage his own affairs, he was also known, and very well known, for a man with a singular talent for managing the affairs of the community; he could manage successfully, for example, town meetings and every sort of business, great or small, incidental to local politics. This talent he may have inherited from his father, who was himself a notable of the neighborhood — one of the organizers of the "New South" church, and prominent about 1724 in a club popularly known

as the "Caulkers' Club," formed for the purpose of
laying "plans for introducing certain persons into
places of trust and power," and was himself from
time to time introduced into such places of trust
and power as justice of the peace, deacon, select-
man, and member of the provincial assembly.
From an early age, the younger Samuel exhibited
a marked aptitude for this sort of activity, and
was less likely to be found "in his counting-house
a-counting of his money" than in some hospitable
tavern or back shop discussing town topics with
local worthies.   Samuel Adams was born to serve
on committees.   He had the innate slant of mind
that properly belongs to a moderator of mass
meetings called to aggravate a crisis.   With the
soul of a Jacobin, he was most at home in clubs,
secret clubs of which everyone had heard and
few were members, designed at best to accomplish
some particular good for the people, at all events
meeting regularly to sniff the approach of tyranny
in the abstract, academically safeguarding the
commonwealth by discussing the first principles
of government.

From the days of Anne Hutchinson, Boston
never lacked clubs; and the Caulkers' Club was
the prototype of many, rather more secular and

political than religious or transcendental, which flourished in the years preceding the Revolution. John Adams, in that Diary which tells us so much that we wish to know, gives us a peep inside one of these clubs, the "Caucus Club," which met regularly at one period in the garret of Tom Dawes's house. "There they smoke tobacco till you cannot see from one end of the garret to the other. There they drink flip, I suppose, and there they choose a moderator who puts questions to the vote regularly; and selectmen, assessors, collectors, wardens, fire-wards, and representatives are regularly chosen before they are chosen in the town. Uncle Fairfield, Story, Ruddock, Adams, Cooper, and a *rudis indigestaque moles* of others are members. They send committees to wait on the merchants' club, and to propose and join in the choice of men and measures." The artist Copley, in the familiar portrait by which posterity knows Samuel Adams, chose to represent him in conventional garb, on a public and dramatic occasion, standing erect, eyes flashing and mouth firm-set, pointing with admonitory finger to the Charter of Massachusetts Bay — a portrait well suited to hang in the Art Museum or in the meeting place of the Daughters of the Revolution. A

different effect would have been produced if the
man had been placed in Tom Dawes's garret,
dimly seen through tobacco smoke, sitting, with
coat off, drinking flip, in the midst of Uncle
Fairfield, Story, Cooper, and a *rudis indigestaque
moles*. This was his native habitat, an environ-
ment precisely suited to his peculiar talent.

Samuel Adams had a peculiar talent, that indispensable combination of qualities possessed by
all great revolutionists of the crusading type,
such as Jean Jacques Rousseau, John Brown, or
Mazzini. When a man abandons his business or
job and complacently leaves the clothing of his
children to wife or neighbors in order to drink
flip and talk politics, ordinary folk are content to
call him a lazy lout, ne'er-do-well, worthless fellow, or scamp. Samuel Adams was not a scamp.
He might have been no more than a ne'er-do-
well, perhaps, if cosmic forces had not opportunely provided him with an occupation which
his contemporaries and posterity could regard
as a high service to humanity. In his own eyes,
this was the view of the situation which justified
his conduct. When he was about to depart for
the first Continental Congress, a number of friends
contributed funds to furnish him forthwith pre-

sentable apparel: a suit of clothes, new wig, new
hat, "six pair of the best silk hose, six pair of
fine thread ditto, . . . six pair of shoes"; and, it
being "modestly inquired of him whether his fi-
nances were not rather low than otherwise, he
replied it was true that was the case, but *he was
very indifferent about these matters, so that his poor
abilities were of any service to the public;* upon
which the gentleman obliged him to accept a purse
containing about fifteen or twenty Johannes."
To accept so much and still preserve one's self-
respect would be impossible to ordinary men under
ordinary circumstances.   Fate had so ordered the
affairs of Samuel Adams that integrity of character required him to be an extraordinary man
acting under extraordinary circumstances.

The character of his mind, as well as the outward circumstances of his life, predisposed Samuel
Adams to think that a great crisis in the history of
America and of the world confronted the men of
Boston.   There was in him some innate scholastic
quality, some strain of doctrinaire Puritan inheritance diverted to secular interests, that gave direction to all his thinking.   In 1743, upon receiving
the degree of Master of Arts from Harvard College, he argued the thesis. "Whether it be lawful

to resist the Supreme Magistrate, if the Commonwealth cannot otherwise be preserved." We may suppose that the young man acquitted himself well, reasoning with great nicety in favor of the legality of an illegal action, doubtless to the edification of Governor Shirley, who was present and who perhaps felt sufficiently remote from the performance, being himself only an actual supreme magistrate presiding over a real commonwealth. And indeed for most young men a college thesis is but an exercise for sharpening the wits, rarely dangerous in its later effects. But in the case of Samuel Adams, the ability to distinguish the speculative from the actual reality seemed to diminish as the years passed. After 1764, relieved of the pressure of life's anxieties and daily nourishing his mind on premises and conclusions reasonably abstracted from the relative and the conditioned circumstance, he acquired in a high degree the faculty of identifying reality with propositions about it; so that, for example, Liberty seemed threatened if improperly defined, and a false inference from an axiom of politics appeared the same as evil intent to take away a people's rights. Thus it was that from an early date, in respect to the controversy between the colonies and the mother country, Samuel Adams became possessed of settled convictions that were capable of clear and concise presentation and that were at once impersonal and highly subjective, for which outward events — the Stamp Act, the Townshend duties, the appointment of Thomas Hutchinson as Governor, or whatever — furnished as it were the suggestion only, the convictions themselves being largely the result of inward brooding, the finespun product of his own ratiocinative mind.

The crisis which thus threatened — in the mind of Samuel Adams — was not an ordinary one: no mere complication of affairs, or creaking of worn-out institutions, or honest difference of opinion about the expediency or the legality of measures. It was a crisis engendered deliberately by men of evil purpose, public enemies well known and often named. Samuel Adams, who had perhaps not heard of even one of the many materialistic interpretations of history, thought of the past as chiefly instructive in connection with certain great epochal conflicts between Liberty and Tyranny — a political Manicheanism, in which the principle of Liberty was embodied in the virtuous many and the principle of Tyranny in the wicked few. Those who read history must know it for a noto-

rious fact that ancient peoples had lost their liberties at the hands of designing men, leagued and
self-conscious conspirators against the welfare of
the human race.   Thus the yoke was fastened
upon the Romans, "millions . . . enslaved by a
few."   Now, in the year 1771, another of these
epochal conflicts was come upon the world, and
Samuel Adams, living in heroic days, was bound
to stand in the forefront of the virtuous against
"restless Adversaries . . . forming the most dangerous Plans for the Ruin of the Reputation of
the People, in order to build their own Greatness
upon the Destruction of their liberties."

A superficial observer might easily fall into the
error of supposing that the restless adversaries and
designing conspirators against whom patriots had
to contend were all in England; on the contrary,
the most persistent enemies of Liberty were
Americans residing in the midst of the people whom
they sought to despoil.   One might believe that in
England "the general inclination is to wish that
we may preserve our liberties; and perhaps even
the ministry could for some reasons find it in their
hearts to be willing that we should be restored to
the state we were in before the passing of the
Stamp Act."   Even Lord Hillsborough, richly

meriting the "curses of the disinterested and better part of the colonists," was by no means "to be reckoned the most inveterate and active of all the Conspirators against our rights. There are others on this side of the Atlantick who have been more insidious in plotting the Ruin of our Liberties than even he, and they are the more infamous, because the country they would enslave, is that very Country in which (to use the words of their Adulators and Expectants) they were 'born and educated.'" Of all these restless adversaries and infamous plotters of ruin, the chief, in the mind of Samuel Adams, was probably Mr. Thomas Hutchinson.

Judged only by what he did and said and by such other sources of information as are open to the historian, Thomas Hutchinson does not appear to have been, prior to 1771, an Enemy of the Human Race. One of his ancestors, Mistress Anne Hutchinson, poor woman, had indeed been — it was as far back as 1637 — an enemy of the Boston Church; but as a family the Hutchinsons appear to have kept themselves singularly free from notoriety or other grave reproach. Thomas Hutchinson himself was born in 1711 in Garden Court Street, Boston, of rich but honest parents,

a difficult character which he managed for many
years to maintain with reasonable credit. In
1771, he was a grave, elderly man of sixty years,
more distinguished than any of his forebears had
been, having since the age of twenty-six been honored with every important elective and appoint-
ive office in the province, including that of governor, which he had with seeming reluctance just
accepted. It may be that Thomas Hutchinson
was ambitious; but if he elbowed his way into
office by solicitation or by the mean arts of an
intriguer the fact was well concealed. He was
not a member of the "Caulkers' Club." So far
as is known, he was not a member of any club
designed "to introduce certain persons into
places of trust and power"; except indeed of
the club, if one may call it such, composed
of the "best families," closely interrelated by
marriage and social intercourse, mostly wealthy,
enjoying the leisure and the disposition to occupy themselves with affairs, and commonly
regarding themselves as forming a kind of natural aristocracy whose vested duty it was to
manage the commonwealth. To this club Mr.
Hutchinson belonged; and it was no doubt partly
through its influence, without any need of solici-

tation on his part, that offices were thrust upon him.

One morning in September, 1760—it was the day following the death of Chief Justice Sewall—Mr. Hutchinson was stopped in the street by the first lawyer in the province, Jeremiah Gridley, who assured him that he, Mr. Hutchinson, must be Mr. Sewall's successor; and it soon appeared that other principal lawyers, together with the surviving judge of the Superior Court, were of the same opinion as Mr. Gridley. Although the place was an attractive one, Mr. Hutchinson distrusted his ability to discharge competently the duties of a Chief Justice, since he had never had any systematic training as a lawyer. Besides, as he was aware, James Otis, Sr., who desired the place and made no secret of the fact that he had formerly been promised it by Governor Shirley, at once became active in pressing his claims upon the attention of Governor Bernard. In this solicitation he was joined by his son, James Otis, Jr. Mr. Hutchinson, on the contrary, refrained from all solicitation, so he tells us at least, and even warned Governor Bernard that it would perhaps be wiser to avoid any trouble which the Otises might be disposed to make in case they were disappointed.

This line of conduct may have been only a shrewder form of solicitation, the proof of which, to some minds, would be that Mr. Hutchinson was in fact appointed to be Chief Justice. This appointment was afterwards recalled as one of Mr. Hutchinson's many offenses, although at the time it seems to have given general satisfaction, especially to the lawyers.

The lawyers may well have been pleased, for the new Chief Justice was a man whose outstanding abilities, even more than his place in society, marked him for responsible position. Thomas Hutchinson possessed the efficient mind. No one surpassed him in wide and exact knowledge, always at command, of the history of the province, of its laws and customs, of past and present practice in respect to the procedure of administration. Industrious and systematic in his habits of work, conscientious in the performance of his duties down to the last jot and tittle of the law, he was preëminently fitted for the neat and expeditious dispatch of official business; and his sane and trenchant mind, habituated by long practice to the easy mastery of details, was prompt to pass upon any practical matter, however complicated, an intelligent and just judgment. It was doubtless thought, in an age when the law was not too highly specialized to be understood by any but the indoctrinated, that these traits would make him a good judge, as they had made him a good councilor. Not all people, it is true, are attracted by the efficient mind; and Mr. Hutchinson in the course of years had made enemies, among whom were many who still thought of him as the man chiefly responsible for the abolition, some eleven years before, of what was probably the most vicious system of currency known to colonial America. Nevertheless, in the days before the passing of the Stamp Act, Mr. Hutchinson was commonly well thought of, both for character and ability, and might still without offense be mentioned as a useful and honored public servant.

Mr. Hutchinson did not, at any time in his life, regard himself as an Enemy of the Human Race, or of America, or even of liberty rightly considered. Perhaps he had not the fine enthusiasm for the Human Race that Herder or Jean Jacques Rousseau had; but at least he wished it well; and to America, the country in which he was born and educated and in which he had always lived, he was profoundly attached. Of America he was as proud as a cultivated and unbigoted man well could be, extremely jealous of her good name abroad and prompt to stand, in any way that was appropriate and customary, in defense of her rights and liberties. To rights and liberties in general, and to those of America in particular, he had given long and careful thought. It was perhaps characteristic of his practical mind to distinguish the word liberty from the various things which it might conceivably represent, and to think that of these various things some were worth more than others, what any of them was worth being a relative matter depending largely upon circumstances. Speaking generally, liberty in the abstract, apart from particular and known conditions, was only a phrase, a brassy tinkle in Mr. Hutchinson's ear, meaning nothing unless it meant mere absence of all constraint. The liberty which Mr. Hutchinson prized was not the same as freedom from constraint. Not liberty in this sense, or in any sense, but the welfare of a people neatly ordered for them by good government, was what he took to be the chief end of politics; and from this conception it followed that "in a remove from a state of nature to the most perfect state of government there must be a great restraint of natural liberty."

The limitations proper to be placed upon natural liberty could scarcely be determined by abstract speculation or with mathematical precision, but would obviously vary according to the character and circumstances of a people, always keeping in mind the "peace and good order" of the particular community as the prime object. In all such matters reasonable men would seek enlightenment not in the Utopias of philosophers but in the history of nations; and, taking a large view of history, the history more particularly of the British Empire and of Massachusetts Bay, it seemed to Mr. Hutchinson, as it seemed to John Locke and to Baron Montesquieu, that a proper balance between liberty and authority had been very nearly attained in the British Constitution, as nearly perhaps as common human frailty would permit. The prevailing "thirst for liberty," which seemed to be "the ruling passion of the age," Mr. Hutchinson was therefore able to contemplate with much sanity and detachment. "In governments under arbitrary rule" such a passion for liberty might, he admitted, "have a salutary effect; but in governments in which as much freedom is enjoyed as can consist with the ends of government, as was the case in this

Province, it must work anarchy and confusion unless there be some external power to restrain it."

In 1771, Thomas Hutchinson was perfectly convinced that this passion for liberty, during several years rising steadily in the heads of the most unstable part of the population, the most unstable "both for character and estates," had brought Massachusetts Bay to a state not far removed from anarchy. Not that he was unaware of the mistakes of ministers. The measures of Mr. Grenville he had regarded as unwise from every point of view. In behalf of the traditional privileges of the colonies — privileges which their conduct had well justified — and in behalf of the welfare of the Empire, he had protested against these measures, as also later against the measures of Mr. Townshend; and of all these measures he still held the same opinion, that they were unwise measures. Nevertheless, Parliament had undoubtedly a legal right — other rights in the political sense, Mr. Hutchinson knew nothing of — to pass them; and the passing of legal measures, however unwise, was not to his mind clear evidence of a conspiracy to establish absolute despotism on the ruins of English liberty. Mr. Hutchinson was doubtless temperamentally less inclined to fear tyranny than anarchy. Of the two evils, he doubtless preferred such oppression as might result from parliamentary taxation to any sort of liberty the attainment of which might seem to require the looting of his ancestral mansion by a Boston mob. In 1771, at the time of his accession to the governorship, Mr. Hutchinson was therefore of opinion that "there must be an abridgment of *what is called* English liberty."

The liberty Thomas Hutchinson enjoyed least and desired most to have abridged was the liberty of being governed, in that province where he had formerly been happy in the competent discharge of official duties, by a self-constituted and illegal popular government intrenched in the town of Boston. In a letter which he wrote in 1765 but did not send, he said:

It will be some amusement to you to have a more circumstantial account of the model of government among us. I will begin with the lowest branch, partly legislative, partly executive. This consists of the rabble of the town of Boston, headed by one Mackintosh, who, I imagine, you never heard of. He is a bold fellow, and as likely for a Masaniello as you can well conceive. When there is occasion to burn or hang effigies or pull down houses, these are employed; but since government has been brought to a system, they are somewhat controlled by a superior set consisting of the master-masons, and carpenters, &c., of the town of Boston. When anything of more importance is to be determined, as opening the custom-house on any matter of trade, these are under the direction of a committee of the merchants, Mr. Rowe at their head, then Molyneaux, Soloman Davis, &c.: but all affairs of a general nature, opening of the courts of law, &c., this is proper for a general meeting of the inhabitants of Boston, where Otis, with his mob-high eloquence, prevails in every motion, and the town first determine what is necessary to be done, and then apply either to the Governor or Council, or resolve that it is necessary for the General Court to correct it; and it would be a very extraordinary resolve indeed that is not carried into execution.

This was in 1765. In 1770, the matter had ceased to be amusing, for every year the model government was brought to a greater perfection, so that at last the Town Meeting, prescriptively composed of certain qualified voters and confined to the determination of strictly local matters, had not only usurped all the functions of government in the province, which was bad enough, but was completely under the thumb of every Tom, Dick, and Harry who might wish to attend, which was manifestly still worse. "There is a Town Meeting, no sort of regard being had to any qualification of voters, but all the inferior people meet together; and at a late meeting the inhabitants of other towns who happened to be in town, mixed with them, and made, they say themselves, near 3000, — their newspapers say 4000, when it is not likely there are 1500 legal voters in the town. It is in other words being under the government of a mob. This has given the lower part of the people such a sense of their importance that a gentleman does not meet with what used to be common civility, and we are sinking into perfect barbarism. . . . The spirit of anarchy which prevails in Boston is more than I am able to cope with." The instigators of the mob, it was well known, were certain artful and self-seeking demagogues, of whom the chief had formerly been James Otis; but in late years Mr. Otis, "with his mob-high eloquence," had given way to an abler man, Samuel Adams, than whom, Mr. Hutchinson thought, there was not "a greater incendiary in the King's dominion, or a man of greater malignity of heart, [or one] who less scruples any measure however criminal to accomplish his purposes."

The letter, undated and undirected, in which Thomas Hutchinson pronounced this deliberate judgment on Samuel Adams, was probably written

about the time of his accession to the Governorship; that is to say, about the time when Mr.
Johnson, the Connecticut Agent, was writing to
Wedderburn that "the people seem to grow weary
of altercations," and that "a little discreet conduct
on both sides" would perfectly restore cordial relations between Britain and her colonies.   In the
way of "a little discreet conduct," even a very
little, not much was to be hoped for from either
Governor Hutchinson or Samuel Adams in their
dealings with each other.   Unfortunately, they
had dealings with each other: in the performance
of official functions, their incommensurable and
repellent minds were necessarily brought to bear
upon the same matters of public concern.   Both,
unfortunately, lived in Boston and were likely
any day to come face to face round the corner of
some or other narrow street of that small town.
That reciprocal exasperation engendered by reasonable propinquity, so essential to the life of altercations, was therefore a perpetual stimulus to both
men, confirming each in his obstinate opinion of
the other as a malicious and dangerous enemy
of all that men hold dear.   Thus it was that during the years 1771 and 1772, when if ever it appeared that others were "growing weary of alter-

cations," these honorable men and trusted leaders did what they could to perpetuate the controversy. By giving or taking occasion to recall ancient grudges or revive fruitless disputes, wittingly or unwittingly they together managed during this time of calm to keep the dying embers alive against the day when some rising wind might blow them into devouring flames.

With Samuel Adams it was a point of principle to avoid discreet conduct as much as possible. In his opinion, the great crisis which was his soul's abiding place, wherein he nourished his mind and fortified his will, admitted of no compromise. Good will was of no avail in dealing with the "Conspirators against our Liberties," the very essence of whose tactics it was to assume the mask of benevolence, and so divide, and by dividing disarm, the people; "flattering those who are pleased with flattery; forming connections with them, introducing Levity, Luxury, and Indolence, and assuring them that if they are quiet the Ministry will alter their Measures." During these years there was no power in the course of events or in the tongue of man to move him in the conviction that "if the Liberties of America are ever completely ruined, it will in all probability be the consequence of a mistaken notion of *prudence,* which leads men to acquiesce in measures of the most destructive tendency for the sake of present ease." Never, therefore, were "the political affairs of America in a more dangerous state" than when the people had seemingly grown weary of altercations and Parliament could endure an entire session "without one offensive measure." The chief danger of all was that the people would think there was no danger. Millions could never be enslaved by a few "if all possessed the independent spirit of *Brutus* who to his immortal honor *expelled the proud Tyrant of Rome.*" During the years of apathy and indifference Samuel Adams accordingly gave his days and nights, with undiminished enthusiasm and a more trenchant acerbity, to the task of making Brutuses of the men of Boston that the fate of Rome might not befall America.

They were assured in many an essay by this new Candidus that

The liberties of our country, the freedom of our civil constitution, are worth defending at all hazards: and it is our duty to defend them against all attacks. We have received them as a fair inheritance from our worthy ancestors. They purchased them for us with toil and danger and expense of treasure and blood; and transmitted them to us with care and diligence. It will bring an everlasting mark of infamy upon the present generation, enlightened as it is, if we should suffer them to be wrested from us by violence without a struggle; or be cheated out of them by the artifices of false and designing men. Of the latter we are in most danger at present. Let us therefore be aware of it. Let us contemplate our forefathers and posterity; and resolve to maintain the rights bequeathed to us from the former, for the sake of the latter. Instead of sitting down satisfied with the efforts we have already made, *which is the wish of our enemies,* the necessity of the times, more than ever, calls for our utmost circumspection, deliberation, fortitude and perseverance. Let us remember that " if we suffer tamely a lawless attack upon our liberty, we encourage it, and involve others in our doom!" It is a very serious consideration, which should deeply impress our minds, that *millions yet unborn may be the miserable sharers in the event.*

These were days when many a former Brutus seemed ready to betray the cause. Deserted by James Otis, whom he had supplanted, and by John Hancock, whose great influence he had formerly exploited and whom he had "led about like an ape," as was currently reported, Samuel Adams suffered a measure of eclipse. The Assembly would no longer do his bidding in respect to the vital question of whether the General

Court might be called by the Governor to meet
outside of Boston; and it even imposed upon him,
as one of a committee, the humiliating task of
presenting an address to Mr. Hutchinson, ac-
knowledging his right to remove the legislature to
any place he liked — "to Housatonic, in the western extreme of the province," if he thought fit.
There was even grave danger that the Governor
would be satisfied with this concession and would
recall the Court to sit in Boston.   Boston was
indeed the very place where Samuel Adams wished
to have it sit; but to attain a right end in a wrong
manner would be to suffer a double defeat, losing
at once the point of principle and the grievance
necessary for maintaining the contention.   Friends
of the Government were much elated at the waning influence of the Chief Incendiary; and Mr.
Sparhawk condescended to express a certain sympathy for their common enemy, now that he was so
much diminished, "harassed, dependent, in their
power."   It was indeed under great difficulties,
during these years when Massachusetts was almost without annals, that Samuel Adams labored
to make Brutuses of the men of Boston.

So far deserted by his friends, Samuel Adams
might never have succeeded in overcoming these

difficulties without the assistance presently rendered by his enemies. Of those who were of
invaluable aid to him in this way, Thomas Hutchinson was one. The good Governor, having read
his instructions, knew what his duties were. One
of them manifestly was to stand in defense of
Government; and, when Government was every
day being argumentatively attacked, to provide,
as a counter-irritant, arguments in defense of Government. Imagining that facts determined conclusions and conclusions directed conduct, Mr.
Hutchinson hoped to diminish the influence of
Samuel Adams by showing that the latter's facts
were wrong, and that his inferences, however
logically deduced, were therefore not to be taken
seriously. "I have taken much pains," he says,
"to procure writers to answer the pieces in the
newspapers which do so much mischief among
the people, and have two or three engaged with
Draper, besides a new press, and a young printer
who says he will not be frightened, and I hope for
some good effect."

The Governor had read his instructions, but
not the mind of Samuel Adams or the minds of
the many men who, like the Chief Incendiary,
were prepared "to cultivate the sensations of

freedom." Perhaps the only "good effect" of his "pieces" was to furnish excellent theses for Samuel Adams to dispute upon, which he did with unrivaled shrewdness each week in the *Boston Gazette* under the thin disguise of Candidus, Valerius Poplicola, or Vindex. To this last name, Vindex, Mr. Hutchinson thought there might appropriately have been added another, such as Malignus or Invidus. And indeed of all these disputative essays, in the *Boston Gazette* or in Mr. Draper's paper, one may say that the apparent aim was to win a dialectic victory and the obvious result to prove that ill will existed by exhibiting it.

Thomas Hutchinson's faith in the value of disputation was not easily disturbed; and after two years, when it appeared that his able lieutenants writing in Mr. Draper's newspaper were still as far as ever from bringing the controversy to a conclusion, he could no longer refrain from trying his own practiced hand at an argument — which he did in a carefully prepared address to the General Court, delivered January 6, 1773. "I have pleased myself for several years," he said, "with hopes that the cause [of the "present disturbed and disordered state" of government] would cease of itself, and the effect with it, but I am disappointed; and I may not any longer, consistent with my duty to the King, and my regard to the interests of the province, delay communicating my sentiments to you upon a matter of so great importance." The cause of their present difficulties Mr. Hutchinson thought as evident as the fact itself: a disturbed state of government having always followed, must have been caused by the denial of the authority of Parliament to make laws binding the province. Upon a right resolution of this question everything depended.

The Governor accordingly confined himself to presenting, all in good temper, a concise and remarkably well-articulated argument to prove that "no line can be drawn between the supreme authority of Parliament and the total independence of the colonies"; of which argument the conclusion must be, inasmuch as the total independence of the colonies was not conceivably any one's thought, that supreme authority rested with Parliament. This conclusion once admitted, it was reasonable to suppose that disturbances would cease; for "if the supremacy of Parliament shall no longer be denied, it will follow that the mere exercise of its authority can be no matter of grievance." In closing, his Excellency expressed the desire, in case the two Houses did not agree with his exposition of the Constitution, to know their objections. "They may be convincing to me, or I may be able to satisfy you of the insufficiency of them. In either case, I hope we shall put an end to those irregularities which ever will be the portion of a government where the supreme authority is controverted." In this roundabout way, Governor Hutchinson finally reached as a conclusion the prepossession with which he began; namely, that whereas a disturbed state of government is, *ex hypothesi*, a vital evil, assertions or denials which tend to cause the evil must be unfounded.

It happened that both Houses, the lower House especially, remained unconvinced by the Governor's exposition of the Constitution; and both Houses took advantage of his invitation to present their objections. The committee which the lower House appointed to formulate a reply found their task no slight one, not from any doubt that Mr. Hutchinson was in error, but from the difficulty of constructing an argument that might be regarded as polemically adequate. At the request of Major Hawley, John Adams was accordingly "invited, requested, and urged to meet the committee, which he did every evening till the report was finished." When the first draft of a reply, probably drawn by Dr. Joseph Warren, was presented to Mr. Adams for his criticism, he "modestly suggested to them the expediency of leaving out many popular and eloquent periods, and of discussing the question with the Governor upon principles more especially legal and constitutional," there being in this first draft, so Mr. Adams thought, "no answer, nor any attempt to answer the Governor's legal and constitutional arguments, such as they were." And so, being "very civilly requested" by the committee to make such changes in the draft as seemed to him desirable, Mr. Adams "drew a line over the most eloquent parts of the oration they had before them, and introduced those legal and historical authorities which appear on the record."

The reply, prepared in this way and finally adopted by the Assembly, was longer and more erudite than Mr. Hutchinson's address. To meet the Governor's major premise and thus undermine his entire argument, legal precedents and the facts of history were freely drawn upon to prove that the colonies were properly "outside of the Realm," and therefore, although parts of the Empire by virtue of being under the special jurisdiction of the Crown, not subject in all matters to parliamentary legislation. Law and history thus supported the contention, contrary to the Governor's assertion, that a line not only could be but always had been "drawn between the supreme authority of Parliament and the total independence of the colonies." Apart from any question of law or fact, the Assembly thought it of high practical importance that this line should be maintained in the future as in the past; for, "if there be no such line," none could deny the Governor's inference that "either the colonies are vassals of the Parliament, or they are totally independent"; upon which the Assembly would observe only that, "as it cannot be supposed to have been the intention of the parties in the compact that we should be reduced to a state of vassalage, the conclusion is that it was their sense that we were thus independent." With very few exceptions, everyone who was of the patriot way of thinking regarded the Assembly's reply as a complete refutation of the argument presented in Governor Hutchinson's address.

In the Governor's opinion, the disturbed state of government to which he had referred in his address was at this time brought to the highest pitch by the committees of correspondence recently established throughout the province — an event long desired and now brought to pass by Samuel Adams. That something might be done by a coördinated system of local committees was an "undigested thought" that dropped from Adams's mind while writing a letter to Arthur Lee in September, 1771. At that time, such was the general apathy of the people, it would clearly "be an arduous task for any man to attempt to awaken a sufficient Number in the colonies to so grand an undertaking." But Samuel Adams, who thought "nothing should be despaired of," took upon himself the performance of this arduous task. Such committees, if they were anywhere needed, were certainly needed in Massachusetts, where the people labored under a "state of perfect Despotism," daily submitting to be ruled by a native Governor who refused to accept a grant from the General Court, received his salary from London, and governed the province according to his instructions. "Is it not enough," asked Valerius Poplicola in the *Gazette*, "to have a Governor . . . *pen-*

sioned by those on whom his existence depends?
. . . Is Life, Property, and Every Thing dear and
sacred, to be now submitted to the Decisions of
PENSION'D JUDGES, holding their places during
the pleasure of *such* a Governor, and a Council
perhaps overawed?"

Confronted by so unprecedented a situation,
it occurred to Samuel Adams that perhaps Mr.
Hutchinson himself might be induced to come to
his assistance. Late in 1772 he accordingly got
the Boston town meeting to present to the Governor an address expressing great alarm at the establishment of salaries for judges, and praying that
the legislature, which was to meet the 2d of December, might not be prorogued. It was possible
that in replying the Governor might take a "high
tone," refusing the request as an interference with
his own prerogative; but, as it was clearly the
right of the people to petition, for the Governor
to refuse would be, Samuel Adams thought, to
"put himself *in the wrong*, in the opinion of every
honest and sensible man; the consequence of which
will be that such measures as the people may
determine upon to save themselves . . . will be
the more reconcilable even to cautious minds, and
thus we may expect that unanimity which we wish

for." The Governor, in a tone that might be called "high," did in fact object to the request as not properly a function of town meetings and thus furnished the occasion for organizing the committees which he thought so disturbing to the state of government.

It was on November 2, 1772, upon a motion of Samuel Adams, that a committee was appointed by a town meeting in Faneuil Hall "to state the Rights of the colonies and of this Province in particular, as Men, as Christians, and as Subjects; to communicate and publish the same to the several Towns in this Province and to the World as the sense of this Town, with the Infringements and Violations thereof that have been, or from time to time may be made . . . requesting of each Town a free communication of their Sentiments on this Subject." The report of the committee, adopted November 20, announced to the world that, as men, the colonists, and those of Massachusetts in particular, were possessed of certain "Natural Rights," among them the right to life, liberty, and property; and that, inasmuch as "men enter into Society . . . by voluntary consent," they still retained "every Natural Right not expressly given up or by the nature of the So-

cial Compact necessarily ceded." Being Christians
as well as men, the colonists enjoyed also those
rights formulated in "the institutes of the great
Lawgiver and head of the Christian Church, . . .
written and promulgated in the New Testament."
Lastly, being Englishmen, the colonists were, "by
the Common Law of England, *exclusive of all
charters from the Crown*, . . . entitled, and by the
acts of the British Parliament . . . declared to
be entitled to all the Liberties and Privileges
of Subjects born . . . within the Realm." The
infringements which had been made upon these
rights, although well known, were once more
stated at length; and all the towns of the province were requested, in case they agreed with the
sentiments of the Town of Boston, to unite in a
common effort "to rescue from impending ruin
our happy and glorious Constitution." For its
part, the Town of Boston was confident that the
wisdom of the other towns, as well as their regard
for themselves and the rising generation, would
not suffer them "to dose, or set supinely indifferent on the brink of destruction, while the Iron
hand of oppression is daily tearing the choicest
Fruit from the fair Tree of Liberty."

Moderate men might think, in the winter of

1773, that "the Iron hand of oppression tearing the choicest Fruit from the Fair Tree of Liberty" was a figure of speech which did not shape itself with nice flexibility to the exact form and pressure of observable facts. It is the limitation of moderate men to be much governed by observable facts; and if the majority could not at once rise to the rhetoric of Samuel Adams, it was doubtless because they had not his instinctive sense of the Arch Conspirator's truly implacable enmity to America. The full measure of this enmity Mr. Adams lived in the hope of some day revealing.

It was of course well known that Mr. Bernard had formerly written home letters most injurious to the province; and in 1770 there "was abundant reason to be jealous," as Samuel Adams, writing on behalf of the Town of Boston, assured Benjamin Franklin, "that the most mischievous and virulent accounts have been lately sent to Administration from Castle William," no doubt from the Commissioners of the Customs. Conveying malicious and unfounded misrepresentations of America under the seal of official correspondence had indeed long been a favorite means of mending the fortunes of those decayed gentlemen and bankrupt politicians whose ambition it was to rise in office by playing the sycophant to some great man in England. Mr. Bernard had "played this game," and had been found out at it, as every one knew. But Mr. Bernard was no American; and it was scarcely to be imagined that Mr. Hutchinson, who boasted "that his Ancestors were of the first Rank and figure in the Country, who . . . had all the Honors lavished upon him which his Fellow-Citizens had it in their power to bestow, who professed the strongest attachment to his native Country and the most tender feelings for its Rights, . . . should be so lost to all sense of Gratitude and public Love as to aid the Designs of despotick power for the sake of rising a single step higher."

This was indeed scarcely to be imagined, yet Samuel Adams imagined it perfectly. Before there was any material evidence of the fact, he was able, by reasonable inference, to erect well-grounded suspicions into a kind of working hypothesis. Mr. Hutchinson, Governor of the Province, was an Enemy of Liberty with many English friends; he would be required by official duty and led by personal inclination to maintain a regular correspondence with high officials in England; from which the conclusion was that

Thomas Hutchinson, professed friend of America, was a traitor, in secret alienating the affections of the King from his loyal subjects.   Samuel Adams knew this well; and now, after all these years, the material evidence necessary to convince men of little faith was at hand.   Under circumstances that might be regarded as providential, Thomas Hutchinson was at last unmasked.

The prelude to this dramatic performance was pronounced in the Massachusetts Assembly, one day in June, 1773, by Mr. John Hancock, who darkly declared that within eight and forty hours a discovery of great pith and moment would be made to the House.   On the next day but one, Samuel Adams arose and desired the galleries cleared, as there were matters to lay before the members which the members only had a right to know of.   When the galleries were cleared he informed the House that certain letters, written by high officials in the province and extremely hostile to the rights and liberties of America, had been procured in England and transmitted to a gentleman who had in turn placed them in his, Mr. Adams's, hands, but with the strictest injunction that they be returned without being copied or printed.   Mr. Adams had given his pledge to this

13

effect; and, if the House would receive them on these terms, he would be glad to read the letters, no restriction having been placed on their being read. They were read accordingly; and a committee having been appointed to make recommendations, it was at length resolved by the House of Assembly that certain letters presented to it by Mr. Samuel Adams tended and were manifestly designed to undermine the Constitution and establish a despotic power in the province. The proceedings of the House being spread abroad, it soon became everywhere known that only the pledged word of the House stood in the way of revelations highly damaging to the public character of Governor Hutchinson.

This outcome of the matter, however gratifying to Samuel Adams, did not satisfy Governor Hutchinson. After there had been "buzzed about for three or four months a story of something that would amaze everybody," and these dark rumors being "spread through all the towns in the province and everybody's expectations . . . raised," it was exasperating to his pragmatic nature to have nothing more definite transpire than that the something which would amaze everybody would indeed amaze everybody if only it could be made known. It should at least be made known to the person most concerned. The Governor therefore requested the Assembly to furnish him copies of the letters which were attributed to him and declared by the House to be destructive of the Constitution. In reply, the House sent certain dates only. The House was of opinion that the Governor could easily make authentic copies of whatever letters he had written at these dates, if he had written any; and such copies, being furnished to the Assembly, might be published, and the whole matter thus cleared up without violating the pledged word of anyone.

With this request the Governor refused to comply, on the ground that it would be improper to reveal his private correspondence and contrary to instructions to reveal that of a public nature. He would say, however, that he had written letters on the days mentioned, but in these letters there was no statement of fact or expression of opinion not already well known. What his opinions were the Assembly and the world might very well gather from his published speeches and his *History of Massachusetts Bay*. It could scarcely be maintained that he had ever lacked frankness in the expression of his opinions; and while his opinions might be thought destructive of the Constitution, it was rather late to be amazed at them. In any case, the Assembly was assured by the Governor that his letters neither tended "nor were designed to subvert, but rather to preserve entire the constitution of government" as established by the charter of the province.

A great many people besides the Governor desired to see letters the substance of which could be so differently understood. Samuel Adams probably preferred not to be forced to print them· knowing their contents, he may have thought that here was a case of those "dangers which, being known, lose half their power for evil"; besides, having pledged his word, he wished to keep it. Yet the pressure of public opinion, becoming every day greater, was difficult to resist, particularly by men who were firm believers in the wisdom of the people. Moreover, it presently appeared that there was no longer any point in refusing to publish the letters, inasmuch as Mr. Hancock assured the House that men on the street were, in some way not known, possessed of copies, some of which had been placed in his hands. Mr. Hancock's copies being found on comparison to be accurate rescripts of the letters which had been read in the House, a committee was accordingly appointed to consider how the House might come into honorable possession of the originals; from which committee Mr. Hawley soon reported that Samuel Adams had informed them that the gentleman from whom he had received the letters now consented to their being copied, seeing that they had already been copied, and printed, seeing that they were already widely circulated; whereupon the House, considering itself in honorable possession, ordered the letters all published.

Nevertheless it was thought expedient, before issuing the letters, to print and circulate such a series of "Resolves" as might prepare the public mind for what was to come later. This was accordingly done. The "Resolves," bearing date of June 16, 1773, indicated clearly and at length the precise significance of the letters; declared it to be the humble opinion of the House that it was not to the interest of the Crown to continue in high places persons "who are known to have, with great industry, though secretly, endeavored to undermine, alter, and overthrow the Constitution of the province"; and concluded by praying "that his Majesty would be pleased to remove

. . . forever from the government thereof" the Honorable Andrew Oliver and his Excellency Thomas Hutchinson.

His Majesty did not remove Mr. Hutchinson; but the Governor's usefulness, from every point of view, was at an end. When the notorious letters were finally printed, it appeared that there were seventeen in all, of which six were written by Mr. Hutchinson in the years 1768 and 1769. These latter documents did not in fact add anything to the world's stock of knowledge; but they had been so heralded, ushered in with so much portentous explication that they scarcely needed to be read to be understood. "Had they been Chevy Chase," the Governor said, the people would have believed them "full of evil and treason." It was indeed the perfect fruit of Samuel Adams's labors that the significance of Mr. Hutchinson's letters had in some manner become independent of their contents. So awake were the people to the danger of being deceived, that whatever the Governor now said or ever had written was taken to be but the substance of things hoped for, the evidence of things not seen.

Meanwhile, the attention of all patriots was diverted from the letters to a far more serious

matter; and when, on December 16, 1773, a cargo
of the East India Company's tea, consigned among
others to Thomas and Elisha Hutchinson, was
thrown into Boston harbor, the great crisis, which
Samuel Adams had done so much to make in-
evitable by virtue of thinking it so, was at last a
reality. It was a limitation of Thomas Hutchinson's excellent administrative mind that he was
wholly unaware of this crisis. In February of the
next year, finding that "a little discreet conduct,"
or indeed any conduct on his part, was altogether
without good effect, the Governor announced that
he had "obtained leave from the King to go to England." On the 1st of June, driving from his home
to the foot of Dorchester Heights, he embarked
on the *Minerva* and arrived in London one month
later. It was his expectation that after a brief
absence, when General Gage by a show of military
force should have brought the province to a reasonable frame of mind, he would return and assume
again the responsibilities of his office. He never
returned, but died in England on June 3, 1780, an
unhappy and a homesick exile from the country
which he loved.

CHAPTER VI

TESTING THE ISSUE

The die is now cast; the colonies must either submit or triumph.
George III.

We hold these truths to be self-evident: that all men are created equal, that they are endowed by their Creator with certain inalienable Rights, that among these are Life, Liberty, and the pursuit of Happiness.

Thomas Jefferson.

Two months and ten days after Mr. Hutchinson embarked for England, John Adams, the Hon. Thomas Cushing, Mr. Samuel Adams, and Robert Treat Paine set out "from Boston, from Mr. Cushing's house, and rode to Coolidge's, where they dined . . . with a large company of gentlemen, who went out and prepared an entertainment for them at that place. A most kindly and affectionate meeting we had, and about four in the afternoon we took leave of them, amidst the kindest wishes and fervent prayers of every man in the company for our health and success. The scene was truly affecting, beyond all description affecting." The four men who in this manner left Boston on the 10th of August, 1774, were bound for Philadelphia to attend the first Continental Congress. Even Samuel Adams, in excellent spirits, a little resplendent and doubtless a little uncomfortable in his new suit and new silk hose, could scarcely have known that they were about to share in one of the decisive events in the history of the modern world.

The calling of the Continental Congress had followed hard upon those recent measures of the British Government which no reasonable man could doubt were designed to reduce the colonies to a state of slavery. In May, 1773, the East India Company, whose privileges in India had just been greatly restricted, was given permission to export tea from its English warehouses directly to America, free of all English customs and excise duties. The threepenny duty in America was indeed retained; but this small tax would not prevent the Company from selling its teas in America at a lower price than other importers, either smugglers or legitimate traders, could afford. It was true the Americans were opposed to the threepenny tax, and they had bound themselves not to import any dutied tea; yet neither the opposition to the tax nor the non-importation agreements entered into had prevented American merchants from importing, during the last three years, about 580,831 pounds of English tea, upon which the duty had been paid without occasioning much comment.

With these facts in mind, hard-headed American merchants, to whom the Company applied for information about the state of the tea trade in the colonies, assured the directors that the Americans drank a great deal of tea, which hitherto had been largely smuggled from Holland; and that, although they were in principle much opposed to the tax, "mankind in general are bound by interest," and "the Company can afford their teas cheaper than the Americans can smuggle them from foreigners, which puts the success of the design beyond a doubt."

The hard-headed merchants were doubtless much surprised at the universal outcry which was raised when it became known that the East India Company was preparing to import its teas into the colonies; and yet the strenuous opposition everywhere exhibited rather confirmed than refuted the philosophical reflection that "mankind in general are bound by interest." Neither the New York and Philadelphia merchants who smuggled tea from Holland, nor the Boston and Charleston merchants who imported dutied tea from England, could see any advantage to them in having this profitable business taken over by the East India Company. Mr. Hancock, for example, was one of the Boston merchants who imported a good deal of dutied tea from England, a fact which was better known then than it has been since; and at Philadelphia John Adams was questioned rather closely about Mr. Hancock's violation of the non-importation agreement, in reply to which he could only say: "Mr. Hancock, I believe, is justifiable, but I am not certain whether he is strictly so." Justifiable or not, Mr. Hancock would not wish to see the entire tea trade of America in the hands of the East India Company.

And indeed to whose interest would it be to have an English company granted a monopoly of a thriving branch of American trade? To those, doubtless, who were the consignees of the Company, such as the sons of Thomas Hutchinson, or Mr. Abram Lott of New York. Certainly no private merchant "who is acquainted with the operation of a monopoly . . . will send out or order tea to America when those who have it at first hand send to the same market." And therefore, since the Company have the whole supply, America will "ultimately be at their mercy to extort what price they please for their tea. And when they find their success in this article, they will obtain liberty to export their spices, silks, etc." This was the light in which the matter appeared to the New York Committee of Correspondence.

John Dickinson saw the matter in the same light, a light which his superior abilities enabled him to portray in more lurid colors. The conduct of the East India Company in Asia, he said,

has given ample proof how little they regard the laws of nations, the rights, liberties, or lives of men. They have levied war, excited rebellions, dethroned princes, and sacrificed millions for the sake of gain. The revenues of mighty kingdoms have centered in their coffers. And these not being sufficient to glut their avarice, they have, by the most unparalleled barbarities, extortions, and monopolies, stripped the miserable inhabitants of their property and reduced whole provinces to indigence and ruin . . . Thus having drained the sources of that immense wealth . . . they now, it seems, cast their eyes on America, a new theater, whereon to exercise their talents of rapine, oppression, and cruelty. The monopoly of tea, is, I dare say, but a small part of the plan they have formed to strip us of our property. But thank God we are not Sea Poys, nor Marattas, but British subjects, who are born to liberty, who know its worth, and who prize it high.

For all of these reasons, therefore — because they were in principle opposed to taxation without consent, and by interest opposed to an English company monopolizing the tea trade, and perhaps because they desired to give a signal demonstration of the fact that they were neither Sea Poys nor Marattas — Americans were willing to resort to the use of force in order to maintain their own rights by depriving the East India Company of its privileges.

When Capt. Curling's ship arrived in Charleston, the people in that town, assembled to deal with the grave crisis, were somewhat uncertain what to do with the Company's tea. On the very ship which brought the Company's tea, there were some chests consigned to private merchants; and certain enthusiastic patriots attending the meeting of citizens affirmed that the importation of dutied tea by private merchants contrary to the non-importation agreement was no less destructive to liberty than the importation of tea by the East India Company. "All this," it was said, "evinced a desire of not entering hastily into measures." In the end, the Company's tea was seized by the Collector and stored in the vaults under the Exchange. At New York and Philadelphia, the Company's tea ships were required to return to England without landing; and it was only at Boston, where Governor Hutchinson, whose sons had been appointed by the Company as its consignees, refused return clearance papers, that the tea, some £14,000 worth of it, was thrown into the harbor.

Throwing the tea into the harbor raised a sharp sense of resentment in the minds of Britons. The common feeling was that, unless the British Government was prepared to renounce all pretense of governing the colonies, something must be done. There were a few, such as Josiah Tucker, who thought that the thing to do was to give up the colonies; in their opinion, colonies were in any case more of a burden than an advantage, the supposed advantages of colonies being bound up with restrictions on trade, and restrictions on trade being contrary to the natural law by which commerce should be free. But the natural law was only a recent discovery not yet widely accepted in

England; and it did not occur to the average Briton that the colonies should be given up. The colonies, he supposed, were English colonies; and he thought the time had come to establish that fact. He had heard that the colonies had grievances. All he knew was that the Government had good-naturedly made concessions for the last ten years; and as for this new grievance about tea, the average Briton made out only that the Americans could buy their tea cheaper than he could himself.

Obviously the time had come for Old England to set the colonies right by showing less concession and more power. Four regiments, as General Gage said, would do the business. The average Briton therefore gave his cordial approval to four " coercive " measures, passed by overwhelming majorities in Parliament, which remodeled the Massachusetts charter, authorized the Governor to transfer to courts in other colonies or to England any cases involving a breach of the peace or the conduct of public officers, provided for quartering troops on the inhabitants, and closed the port of Boston until the East India Company should have been compensated for the loss of it, tea. In order to make these measures effective

General Gage, commander of the American forces, was made Governor of Massachussetts. To what extent he would find it necessary to use the military depended upon the Bostonians. "The die is now cast," the King wrote to Lord North; "the colonies must either submit or triumph." The King's judgment was not always good; but it must be conceded that in this instance he had penetrated to the very center of the situation.

Massachusetts, very naturally, wished not to submit, but whether she could triumph without the support of the other colonies was more than doubtful; and it was to obtain this support, to devise if possible a method of resistance agreeable to all, that the Congress was now assembling at Philadelphia. The spirit in which the colonies received the news of the Boston Port Bill augured well for union, for in every colony it was felt that this was a challenge which could not be evaded without giving the lie to ten years of high talk about the inalienable rights of Englishmen. As Charles James Fox said, "all were taught to consider the town of Boston as suffering in the common cause." This sentiment John Adams found everywhere expressed — found everywhere, as he took his leisurely journey southward, that people

were "very firm" in their determination to support Massachusetts against the oppression of the
British Government.

In respect to the measures which should be
adopted to achieve the end desired, there was not
the same unanimity. Mr. Adams, at the age of
thirty-eight years, never having been out of New
England, kept his eyes very wide open as he
entered the foreign colonies of New York and
Pennsylvania. In New York he was much im-
pressed with the "elegant country seats," with
the bountiful hospitality, and the lavish way of
living. "A more elegant breakfast I never saw" —
this was at Mr. Scott's house — "rich plate, a very
large silver coffee-pot, a very large silver tea-pot,
napkins of the finest materials, toast, and bread
and butter in great perfection," and then, to top
it off, "a plate of beautiful peaches, another of
pears, and another of plums, and a musk-melon
were placed upon the table." Nevertheless, in
spite of the friendliness shown to him personally,
in spite of the sympathy which, abstractly considered, the New Yorkers expressed for the sad
state of Boston, Mr. Adams was made to understand that if it came to practical measures for the
support of Massachusetts, many diverse currents

of opinion and interest would make themselves felt.

New York was "very firm" in the cause, certainly, but "Mr. MacDougall gave a caution to avoid every expression which looked like an allusion to the last appeal. He says there is a powerful party here who are intimidated by fears of a civil war, and they have been induced to acquiesce by assurances that there was no danger, and that a peaceful cessation of commerce would effect relief. Another party, he says, are intimidated lest the leveling spirit of the New England colonies should propagate itself into New York. Another party are instigated by Episcopalian prejudices against New England. Another party are merchants largely concerned in navigation, and therefore afraid of non-importation, non-consumption, and non-exportation agreements. Another party are those who are looking up to Government for favors."

These interests were doubtless well enough represented by the New York deputies to the Congress, whom Mr. Adams now saw for the first time. Mr. Jay, it was said, was a good student of the law and a hard worker. Mr. Low, "they say, will profess attachment to the cause of liberty, but his sincerity is doubted." Mr. Alsop was thought to be of good heart, but unequal, as Mr. Scott affirmed, "to the trust in point of abilities." Mr. Duane — this was Mr. Adams's own impression — "has a sly, surveying eye, . . . very sensible, I think, and very artful." And finally there was Mr. Livingston, "a downright, straightforward man," who reminded Mr. Adams that Massachusetts had once hung some Quakers, affirmed positively that civil war would follow the renunciation of allegiance to Britain, and threw out vague hints of the Goths and Vandals.

Confiding these matters to his *Diary* and keeping his own opinion, Mr. Adams passed on to Philadelphia. There the Massachusetts men were cordially welcomed, twice over, but straightway cautioned against two gentlemen, one of whom was "Dr. Smith, the Provost of the College, who is looking up to Government for an American Episcopate and a pair of lawn sleeves" — a very soft, polite man, "insinuating, adulating, sensible, learned, insidious, indefatigable," with art enough, "and refinement upon art, to make impressions even upon Mr. Dickinson and Mr. Reed." In Pennsylvania, as in every colony, Mr. Adams found, there was a tribe of people "exactly like the tribe, in the Massachusetts, of Hutchinsonian Addressers." Some of this tribe had managed to elbow their way into the committees of deputies to the Congress, at least from the middle colonies, and probably from South Carolina as well.

The "most spirited and consistent of any" of the deputies were the gentlemen from Virginia, among whom were Mr. Henry and Mr. R. H. Lee, said to be the Demosthenes and the Cicero of America. The latter, Mr. Adams liked much, a "masterly man" who was very strong for the most vigorous measures. But it seemed that even Mr. Lee was strong for vigorous measures only because he was "absolutely certain that the same ship which carries hence the resolutions will bring back the redress." If he supposed otherwise, he "should be for exceptions."

From the first day of the Congress it was known that the Massachusetts men were in favor of "vigorous measures," vigorous measures being understood to mean the adoption of strict non-importation, non-consumption, and non-exportation agreements. There were moments when John Adams thought even these measures tame and unheroic: "When Demosthenes (God forgive

the vanity of recollecting his example) went
ambassador from Athens to the other states of
Greece, to excite a confederacy against Phillip,
he did not go to propose a Non-Importation or
Non-Consumption Agreement. . . ." For all
this, the Massachusetts men kept themselves well
in the background, knowing that there was much
jealousy and some fear of New England leadership
and well aware that the recent experience with
non-importation agreements had greatly diminished, in the mercantile colonies of New York,
Pennsylvania, and South Carolina, the enthusiasm
for such experiments.

The trouble with non-importation agreements,
as Major Hawley had told John Adams, was that
"they will not be faithfully observed; that the
Congress have no power to enforce obedience to
their laws; that they will be like a legislative without an executive." Did Congress have, or could
it assume, authority to compel men to observe its
resolutions, to compel them to observe, for example, a non-importation agreement? This was a
delicate question upon which opinion was divided.
"We have no legal authority," said Mr. Rutledge,
"and obedience to our determinations will only
follow the reasonableness, the apparent utility, and

necessity of the measures we adopt. We have no coercive or legislative authority." If this was so, the non-intercourse policy would doubtless prove a broken reed. Massachusetts men were likely to be of another opinion, were likely to agree with Patrick Henry, who affirmed that "Government is dissolved. Fleets and armies and the present state of things show that government is dissolved. We are in a state of nature, Sir!" If they were indeed in a state of nature, it was perhaps high time that Congress should assume the powers of a government, in which case it might be possible to adopt and to enforce non-intercourse measures. In this gingerly way did the deputies lift the curtain and peer down the road to revolution.

The deputies, like true Britons, contrived to avoid the highly theoretical question of authority, and began straightway to concern themselves with the practical question of whether the Congress, with or without authority, should recommend the adoption of strict non-intercourse agreements. Upon this question, as the chief issue, the deputies were divided into nearly equal groups. Mr. Galloway, Mr. Duane, and Mr. Rutledge were perhaps the leaders of those, probably a majority at first, who were opposed to such vigorous measures, fearing that they were intended as a cloak to cover the essentially revolutionary designs of the shrewd New Englanders. "We have too much reason to suspect that independence is aimed at," Mr. Low warned the Congress; and Mr. Galloway could see that while the Massachusetts men were in "behavior very modest, yet they are not so much so as not to throw out hints, which like straws and feathers show from which point in the compass the wind comes." In the early days of the Congress, if we are to believe Mr. Hutchinson, this cold north wind was so much disliked that the New York and New Jersey deputies, "and others," carried a vote against the adoption of non-intercourse agreements, "agreed to present a petition to the King," and "expected to break up, when letters arrived from Dr. Franklin which put an end to the petition."

The Journals of the Congress do not record any vote of this kind; but a number of things are known to have occurred in the Congress which the Journals do not record. On September 17, the famous "Suffolk Resolves" were laid before the deputies for their approval. The resolutions had been adopted by a county convention in Massa-

chusetts, and in substance they recommended to
the people of Massachusetts to form a government independent of that of which General Gage
was the Governor, urged them meanwhile to arm
themselves in their own defense, and assured them
that "no obedience is due from this province to
either or any part" of the Coercive Acts.   These
were indeed "vigorous measures"; and when the
resolutions came before Congress, "long and warm
debates ensued between the parties," Mr. Galloway afterwards remembered; and he says that
when the vote to approve them was finally carried,
"two of the dissenting members presumed to offer
their protest to it in writing which was negatived,"
and when they then insisted that the "tender of
the protest and the negative should be entered on
the minutes, this was also rejected."

Later in the month, September 28, Mr. Galloway
introduced his famous plan for a "British-American
Parliament" as a method for permanent reconciliation. The motion to enter the plan on the minutes
and to refer it for further consideration gave rise
to "long and warm debates," the motion being
carried by a majority of one colony; but subse-
quently, probably on October 21, it was voted
to expunge the plan, together with all resolution⸳

referring to it, from the minutes. Nothing, as Benjamin Franklin wrote from England, could so encourage the British Government to persist in its oppressive policy as the knowledge that dissensions existed in the Congress; and since these dissensions did unfortunately exist, there was a widespread feeling that it would be the part of wisdom to conceal them as much as possible.

No doubt a majority of the deputies, when they first read the Suffolk Resolutions, were amazed that the rash New Englanders should venture to pledge themselves so frankly to rebellion. Certainly no one who thought himself a loyal subject of King George could even contemplate rebellion; but, on the other hand, to leave Massachusetts in the lurch after so much talk of union and the maintenance of American rights would make loyal Americans look a little ridiculous. That would be to show themselves lambs as soon as Britons had shown themselves lions, which was precisely what their enemies in England boasted they would do. Confronted by this difficult dilemma, moderate men without decided opinions began to fix their attention less upon the exact nature of the measures they were asked to support, and more upon the probable

effect of such measures upon the British Government. It might be true, and all reports from
England seemed to point that way, that the British Government was only brandishing the sword
in terrorem, to see whether the Americans would
not run at once to cover; in which case it would be
wiser for all loyal subjects to pledge themselves
even to rebellion, the prospect being so very good
that Britain would quickly sheathe its sword and
present instead the olive branch, saying, "This is
what I intended to offer." Therefore, rather than
leave Massachusetts in the lurch and so give the
lie to the boasted unity of the colonies, many
moderate and loyal subjects voted to approve the
Suffolk Resolutions, which they thought very rash
and ill-advised measures.

Whatever differences still prevailed, if indeed
practical men could hold out after the accomplished fact, might be bridged and compromised
by adopting those petitions and addresses which
the timid thought sufficient and at the same time
by subscribing to and "recommending" those non-
intercourse agreements which the bolder sort
thought essential.

This compromise was in fact effected. The
Congress unanimously adopted the moderate ad-

dresses which Lord Chatham afterwards praised for their masterly exposition of true constitutional principles; but it likewise adopted, also unanimously, a series of resolutions known as the Association, to which the deputies subscribed their names. By signing the Association, the deputies bound themselves, and recommended the people in all the colonies to bind themselves, not to import, after December 1, 1774, any commodities from Great Britain or Ireland, or molasses, syrups, sugars, and coffee from the British plantations, or East India Company tea from any place, or wines from Madeira, or foreign indigo; not to consume, after March 1, 1775, any of these commodities; and not to export, after September 10, 1775, any commodities whatever to Great Britain, Ireland, or the West Indies, "except rice to Europe." It was further recommended that a committee be formed in each city, town, and county, whose business it should be to observe the conduct of all persons, those who refused to sign the Association as well as those who signed it, and to publish the names of all persons who did not observe the agreements there entered into, "to the end that all such foes of the rights of British-America may be publicly known and universally condemned as the enemies of American liberty"; and it was likewise recommended that the committees should inspect the customs entries frequently, that they should seize all goods imported contrary to the recommendation of the Association and reship them, or, if the owner preferred, sell them at public auction, the owner to be recompensed for the first costs, the profits, if any, to be devoted to relieving the people of Boston.

Having thus adopted a Petition to the King, a Memorial to the Inhabitants of the British Colonies, and an Address to the People of Great Britain, and having recommended a certain line of conduct to be followed by all loyal Americans, the first Continental Congress adjourned. It had assumed no "coercive or legislative authority"; obedience to its determinations would doubtless depend, as Mr. Rutledge had said, upon "the reasonableness, the apparent utility and necessity" of its recommendations.

"There can be no doubt," the Earl of Dartmouth is reported to have said, "that every one who had signed the Association was guilty of treason." The Earl of Dartmouth was not counted one of the enemies of America; and if this was his opinion of the action of the first Continental

Congress, Lord North's supporters in Parliament, a great majority since the recent elections, were not likely to take a more favorable view of it. Nevertheless, when the American question came up for consideration in the winter of 1775, "conciliation" was a word frequently heard on all sides, and even corrupt ministers were understood to be dallying with schemes of accommodation. In January and February great men were sending agents, and even coming themselves, to Dr. Franklin to learn what in his opinion the colonies would be satisfied with. Lord Chatham, as might be guessed, was meditating a plan. On the 29th of January, he came to Craven Street and showed it to Franklin, who made notes upon it, and later went out to Hayes, two hours' ride from London, where he remained for four hours listening to the easy flow of the Great Commoner's eloquence without being able to get any of his own ideas presented.

Fortified by the presence if not by the advice of Franklin, Lord Chatham laid his plan before Parliament on the 1st of February. He would have an explicit declaration of the dependence of the colonies on the Crown and Parliament in all matters of trade and an equally explicit declaration that no tax should be imposed upon the colonies without their consent; and when the Congress at Philadelphia should have acknowledged the supremacy of the Crown and Parliament and should have made a free and perpetual grant of revenue, then he would have all the obnoxious acts passed since 1764, and especially the Coercive Acts, totally repealed.   Lord Sandwich, in a warm speech, moved to reject these proposals at once; and when the vote was taken it was found that 61 noble lords were in favor of rejecting them at once, while only 31 were opposed to so doing.

Lord North was perhaps less opposed to reconciliation than other noble lords were. A few days later Franklin was approached by Admiral Howe, who was understood to know the First Minister's mind, to learn whether he might not suggest something for the Government to go upon. The venerable Friend of the Human Race was willing enough to set down on paper some "Hints" which Admiral Howe might think advisable to show to ministers. It happened, however, that the "Hints" went far beyond anything the Government had in mind. Ministers would perhaps be willing to repeal the Tea Act and the Boston Port Bill; but they felt strongly that the act regulating the Massachusetts charter must stand as "an example of the power of Parliament." Franklin, on the other hand, was certain that "while Parliament claims the right of altering American constitutions at pleasure, there can be no agreement." Since the parties were so far apart, it seemed useless to continue the informal negotiation, and on February 20, Lord North laid before Parliament his own plan for effecting an accommodation.

Perhaps, after all, it was not his own plan; for Lord North, much inclined to regard himself as the King's minister, was likely to subordinate his wishes to those of his master. King George III, at all events, had his own ideas on conciliation. "I am a friend to holding out the olive branch," he wrote in February, "yet I believe that, when vigorous measures appear to be the only means, the colonies will submit." Knowing the King's ideas, as well as those of Dr. Franklin, Lord North accordingly introduced into Parliament the Resolution on Conciliation, which provided that when any colony should make provision "for contributing their proportion to the common defense, . . . and for the support of the civil government, and the administration of justice in such province, . . . it will be proper, . . . for so long as such provision shall be made, . . . to forbear, in respect of such province, . . . to levy any Duty, Tax, or Assessment, . . . except . . . for the regulation of commerce." The minister's resolution, although by most of his supporters thought to be useless, was adopted by a vote of 274 to 88.

It was not the intention of the Government to hold out the olive branch by itself. Lord North, and perhaps the King also, hoped the colonies would accept it; but by all maxims of politics an olive branch was more likely to be accepted if the shining sword was presented at the same time as the only alternative. As early as the 10th of February, Lord North had introduced into Parliament a bill, finally passed March 30, "to restrain the trade and commerce" of the New England colonies to "Great Britain, Ireland, and the British islands in the West Indies," and to exclude these colonies from "carrying on any fishery on the banks of Newfoundland," it being "highly unfit that the inhabitants of the said provinces . . . should enjoy the same privileges of trade . . . to which his Majesty's faithful and obedient subjects are entitled." The provisions of this act were extended to the other colonies in April; and meantime measures were taken to strengthen the naval forces.

The first certain information that Lord North had extended the olive branch reached New York April 24, 1775, two weeks before the day fixed for the meeting of the second Continental Congress. Important changes had taken place since the first Congress, six months earlier, had sent forth its resolutions. In every colony there was a sufficient number of patriots who saw "the reasonableness, the apparent utility, and necessity" of forming the committees which the Association recommended; and these committees everywhere, with a marked degree of success, immediately set about convincing their neighbors of the utility and necessity of signing the non-importation agreement, or at least of observing it even if they were not disposed to sign it. To deny the reasonableness of the Association was now indeed much more difficult than it would have been before the Congress assembled; for the Congress, having published certain resolutions unanimously entered into, had come to be the symbol of America united in defense of its rights; and what American, if indeed one might call him such, would wish to be thought disloyal to America or an enemy of its liberties? It required a degree of assurance for any man to set up his individual judgment against the deliberate and united judgment of the chosen representatives of all the colonies; and that must be indeed a very subtle mind which could draw the distinction between an enemy of liberty and a friend of liberty who was unwilling to observe the Association.

Some such subtle minds there were — a considerable number in most colonies who declared themselves friends of liberty but not of the Association, loyal to America but not to the Congress. One of these was Samuel Seabury, an Episcopalian clergyman living in Westchester County, New York, a vigorous, downright man, who at once expressed his sentiments in a forcible and logical manner, and with much sarcastic humor, in a series of pamphlets which were widely read and much commended by those who found in them their own views so effectively expressed. This Westchester Farmer — for so he signed himself — proclaimed that he had always been, and was still, a friend of liberty in general and of American liberty in particular. The late British measures he thought unwise and illiberal, and he had hoped that the Congress would be able to obtain redress, and perhaps even to effect a permanent reconciliation. But these hopes were seen to be vain from the day when the Congress approved the Suffolk Resolutions and, instead of adopting Mr. Galloway's plan, adopted the Association. For no sane man could doubt that, under the thin disguise of "recommendations," Congress had assumed the powers of government and counseled rebellion. The obvious conclusion from this was that, if one could not be a loyal American without submitting to Congress, then it was impossible to be at the same time a loyal American and a loyal British subject.

But, if the problem were rightly considered, Mr. Seabury thought one might be loyal to America in the best sense without supporting Congress; for, apart from any question of legality, the Association was highly inexpedient, inasmuch as non-importation would injure America more than it injured England, and, for this reason if for no others, it would be found impossible to "bully and frighten the supreme government of the nation." Yet all this was beside the main point, which was that the action of Congress, whether expedient or not, was illegal. It was illegal because it authorized the committees to enforce the Association upon all alike, upon those who never agreed to observe it as well as upon those who did; and these committees, as everyone knew, were so enforcing it and were "imposing penalties upon those who have presumed to violate it." The Congress talked loudly of the tyranny of the British Government. Tyranny! Good Heavens! Was any tyranny worse than that of self-constituted committees which, in the name of liberty, were daily conducting the most hateful inquisition into the private affairs of free British subjects? "Will you choose such committees? Will you submit to them should they be chosen by the weak, foolish, turbulent part of the . . . people? I will not. No. If I must be enslaved, let it be by a KING at least, and not by a parcel of upstart, lawless committee-men."

The Massachusetts men were meanwhile show-ing no disposition to submit to the King. In that colony a Provincial Congress, organized at Salem in October, 1774, and afterwards removed to Cambridge, had assumed all powers of government in spite of General Gage and contrary to the pro-visions of the act by which Parliament had pre-sumed to remodel the Massachusetts charter. Outside of Boston at least, the allegiance of the people was freely given to this extra-legal govern-ment; and under its direction the towns began to prepare for defense by organizing the militia and procuring and storing arms and ammunition.

To destroy such stores of ammunition seemed to General Gage quite the most obvious of his duties; and Colonel Smith was accordingly ordered to proceed to the little village of Concord, some eighteen miles northwest of Boston, and destroy the magazines which were known to be collected there. The night of the 18th of April was the time fixed for this expedition; and in the evening of that day patriots in Boston noted with alarm that bodies of troops were moving towards the waterside. Dr. Joseph Warren, knowing or easily guessing the destination of the troops, at once despatched William Dawes, and later in the evening Paul Revere also, to Lexington and Concord to spread the alarm. As the little army of Colonel Smith — a thousand men, more or less — left Boston and marched up into the country, church bells and the booming of cannon announced their coming. Day was breaking when the British troops approached the town of Lexington; and there on the green they could see, in the early morning light, perhaps half a hundred men standing in military array — fifty against a thousand! The British rushed forward with huzzas, in the midst of which shots were heard; and when the little band of minutemen was dispersed eight of the fifty lay dead upon the village green.

The battle of Lexington was begun, but it was not yet finished. Pushing on to Concord, the thousand disciplined British regulars captured and destroyed the military stores collected there. This was easily done; but the return from Concord to Lexington, and from Lexington to Cambridge, proved a disastrous retreat. The British found indeed no minutemen drawn up in military array to block their path; but they found themselves subject to the deadly fire of men concealed behind the trees and rocks and clumps of shrubs that everywhere conveniently lined the open road. With this method of warfare, not learned in books, the British were unfamiliar. Discipline was but a handicap; and the fifteen hundred soldiers that General Gage sent out to Lexington to rescue Colonel Smith served only to make the disaster greater in the end. When the retreating army finally reached the shelter of Cambridge, it had lost, in killed and wounded, 247 men; while the Americans, of whom it had been confidently asserted in England that they would not stand against British regulars, had lost but 88.

The courier announcing the news of Lexington passed through New York on the 23d of April. Twenty-four hours later, during the height of the excitement occasioned by that event, intelligence arrived from England that Parliament had approved Lord North's Resolution on Conciliation. For extending the olive branch, the time was inauspicious; and when the second Continental Congress assembled, two weeks later, on the 10th of May, men were everywhere wrathfully declaring that the blood shed at Lexington made allegiance to Britain forever impossible.

It might indeed have seemed that the time had come when every man must decide, once for all, whether he would submit unreservedly to the King or stand without question for the defense of America. Yet not all men, not a majority of men in the second Continental Congress, were of that opinion.

The second Congress was filled with moderate minded men who would not believe the time had come when that decision had to be made — men who were bound to sign themselves British-Americans till the last possible moment, many of whom could not now have told whether in the end they would sign themselves Britons or Americans. Surely,

they said, we need not make the decision yet.
We have the best of reasons for knowing that
Britain will not press matters to extremities. Can
we not handle the olive branch and the sword as
well as Lord North? A little fighting, to convince
ministers that we can't be frightened, and all will
be well. We shall have been neither rebels nor
slaves. The second Congress was full of men who
were, as yet, "Neither-Nor."

There was Joseph Galloway, once more elected
to represent Pennsylvania, ready to do what he
could to keep Congress from hasty action, hoping
for the best yet rather expecting the worst, discreetly retiring, at an early date, within the ranks
of the British loyalists. John Alsop, the "soft,
sweet" man, was also there, active enough in his
mild way until the very last — until the Declaration of Independence, as he said, "closed the last
door to reconciliation." There, too, was James
Duane, with never so great need of his "surveying
eye" to enable him to size up the situation. He
is more discreet than any one, and sits quietly in
his seat, on those days when he finds it convenient
to attend, which is not too often — especially after
November, at which time he moved his effects
to Duanesborough, and so very soon disappears

from sight, except perhaps vicariously in the person of his servant, James Brattle, whom we see flitting obscurely from Philadelphia to New York conveying secret information to Governor Tryon. John Jay, the hard-reading young lawyer, who favored Mr. Galloway's plan but in the end signed the Association — here he is again, edging his way carefully along, watching his step, crossing no bridges beforehand, well over indeed before he seems aware of any gulf to be crossed. And here is the famous Pennsylvania Farmer, leader of all moderate men, John Dickinson, only too well aware of the gulf opening up before him, fervently praying that it may close again of its own accord. Mr. Dickinson has no mind for anything but conciliation, to obtain which he will go the length of donning a Colonel's uniform, or at least a Colonel's title, perfecting himself and his neighbors in the manual of arms against the day when the King would graciously listen to the loyal and humble petition of the Congress.

Mr. Dickinson, staking all on the petition, was distressed at the rash talk that went on out of doors; and in this respect, no one distressed him more than his old friend, John Adams, who thought and said that a petition was a waste of time and who was all for the most vigorous measures (such, doubtless, as Demosthenes might have counseled), — the seizure of all crown officers, the formation of state governments, the raising of an army, and negotiations for obtaining the assistance of France.   When Mr. Dickinson, having marshaled his followers from the middle colonies and South Carolina, got his petition before the Congress, John Adams, as a matter of course, made "an opposition to it in as long a speech as I commonly made . . . in answer to all the arguments that had been urged."   And Adams relates in his *Diary* how, being shortly called out of Congress Hall, he was followed by Mr. Dickinson, who broke out upon him in great anger.   "What is the reason, Mr. Adams, that you New-England men oppose our measures of reconciliation?   There now is Sullivan, in a long harangue, following you in a determined opposition to our petition to the King. Look ye!   If you don't concur with us in our pacific system, I and a number of us will break off from you in New England, and we will carry on the opposition by ourselves in our own way."   At that moment it chanced that John Adams was "in a very happy temper" (which was not always the case), and so, he says, was able to reply very coolly. "Mr. Dickinson, there are many things that I can very cheerfully sacrifice to harmony, and even to unanimity; but I am not to be threatened into an express adoption or approbation of measures which my judgment reprobates. Congress must judge, and if they pronounce against me, I must submit, as, if they determine against you, you ought to acquiesce."

The Congress did decide. It decided to adopt Mr. Dickinson's petition; and to this measure John Adams submitted. But the Congress also decided to raise a Continental army to assist Massachusetts in driving the British forces out of Boston, of which army it appointed, as Commander-in-Chief, George Washington, Esq.; and in justification of these measures it published a *Declaration of the Causes and Necessity of Taking up Arms:*

Our cause is just. Our union is perfect. Our internal resources are great, and, if necessary, foreign assistance is undoubtedly attainable. . . . Fortified with these animating reflections, we . . . declare that . . . the arms we have been compelled by our enemies to assume, we will . . . employ for the preservation of our liberties, being with one mind resolved to die freemen rather than live slaves. . . . We have not raised armies with ambitious designs of separating from Great

Britain. . . . We shall lay them down when hostilities shall cease on the part of the aggressors. . . . With an humble confidence in the mercies of the supreme and impartial Judge and Ruler of the Universe, we . . . implore his divine goodness to protect us happily through this great conflict, to dispose our adversaries to reconciliation on reasonable terms, and thereby to relieve the empire from the calamities of civil war.

In these measures Mr. Dickinson acquiesced, as John Adams had submitted to the petition. The "perfect" union which was thus attained was nevertheless a union of wills rather than of opinions; and on July 24, 1775, in a letter to James Warren, John Adams gave a frank account of the state of mind to which the perfect union had reduced him:

In confidence, I am determined to write freely to you this time. A certain great Fortune and piddling Genius, whose Fame has been trumpeted so loudly, has given a silly Cast to our whole Doings. We are between Hawk and Buzzard. We ought to have had in our Hands a month ago the whole Legislative, executive, and judicial of the whole Continent, and have completely modeled a Constitution; to have raised a naval Power, and opened our Ports wide; to have arrested every Friend of Government on the Continent and held them as Hostages for the poor Victims of Boston, and then opened the Door as wide as possible for Peace and Reconciliation. After that they might have petitioned, and negotiated, and addressed, etc., if they would. Is all this extravagant? Is it wild? Is it not the soundest Policy?

It seems that Mr. Adams would have presented the sword boldly, keeping the olive branch carefully concealed behind his back. His letter, intercepted by the British Government, and printed about the time when Mr. Dickinson's petition was received in London, did nothing to make the union in America more perfect, or to facilitate the opening of that refractory "Door . . . for Peace and Reconciliation."

The truth is that John Adams no longer believed in the possibility of opening this door, even by the tiniest crack; and even those who still had faith in the petition as a means to that end found it somewhat difficult to keep their faith alive during the weary month of October while they waited for the King's reply. Mr. Chase, although he had "not absolutely discarded every glimpse of a hope of reconciliation," admitted that the prospect was "gloomy." Mr. Zubly assured Congress that he "did hope for a reconciliation and that this winter may bring it"; and he added, as if justifying himself against sceptical shrugs of shoulders, "I may enjoy my hopes for reconciliation; others

may enjoy theirs that none will take place."
It might almost seem that the idea of reconciliation, in this October of 1775, was a vanishing
image to be enjoyed retrospectively rather than
anything substantial to build upon for the future.
This it was, perhaps, that gave especial point to
Mr. Zubly's oft-repeated assertion that Congress
must speedily obtain one of two things — "a reconciliation with Great Britain, or the means of
carrying on the war."

Reconciliation *or* war! This was surely a new
antithesis. Had not arms been taken up for the
purpose precisely of disposing their adversaries
"to reconciliation on reasonable terms"? Does
Mr. Zubly mean to say then that war is an alternative to reconciliation — an alternative which will
lead the colonies away from compromise towards
that which all have professed not to desire? Is
Mr. Zubly hinting at independence even before
the King has replied to the petition? No. This is
not what Mr. Zubly meant. What he had in the
back of his mind, and what the Congress was
coming to have in the back of its mind, if one
may judge from the abbreviated notes which John
Adams took of the debates in the fall of 1775, was
that if the colonies could not obtain reconciliation

by means of the non-intercourse measures very soon — this very winter as Mr. Zubly hoped — they would have to rely for reconciliation upon a vigorous prosecution of the war; in which case the non-intercourse measures were likely to prove an obstacle rather than an advantage, since they would make it difficult, if not impossible, to obtain the "means of carrying on the war."

The non-intercourse measures had been designed to obtain conciliation by forcing Great Britain to make concessions; but if Great Britain would make no concessions, then the non-intercourse measures, by destroying the trade and prosperity of the colonies, would have no other effect than to bring about conciliation by forcing the colonies to make concessions themselves. This was not the kind of conciliation that any one wanted; and so the real antithesis which now confronted Congress was between war and non-intercourse. Mr. Livingston put the situation clearly when he said: "We are between hawk and buzzard; we puzzle ourselves between the commercial and warlike opposition."

Through long debates Congress puzzled itself over the difficult task of maintaining the Association and of obtaining the means for carrying on the war. Doubtless a simple way out would be for Congress to allow so much exportation only as might be necessary to pay for arms and ammunition; and still not so simple either, since it would at once excite many jealousies. "To get powder," Mr. Jay observed, "we keep a secret law that produce may be exported. Then come the wrangles among the people. A vessel is seen loading — a fellow runs to the committee." Well, it could not be helped; let the fellow run to the committee, and let the committee reassure him — that was the business of the committee; and so the Congress authorized the several colonies to export as much "produce, except horned cattle, sheep, hogs, and poultry, as they may deem necessary for the importation of arms, ammunition, sulphur, and saltpetre." Thus powder might be obtained.

Nevertheless, war could not live by powder alone. The imponderable moral factors had to be considered, chief of which was the popular support or opposition which Congress and the army might count upon under certain circumstances. No doubt people were patriotic and wished to maintain their rights; but no doubt people would be more patriotic and more enthusiastic and practically active in their support of both Congress and the army, if they were reasonably prosperous

and contented than if they were not. Self-
denying ordinances were, by their very nature, of
temporary and limited efficacy; and it was per-
tinent to inquire how long the people would be
content with the total stoppage of trade and the
decay of business which was becoming every day
more marked. "We can live on acorns; but will
we?" It would perhaps be prudent not to expect
"more virtue . . . from our people than any people ever had"; it would be prudent "not to put
virtue to too severe a test, . . . lest we wear it
out." And it might well be asked what would
wear it out and "disunite us more than the decay
of all business? The people will feel, and will say,
that Congress tax them and oppress them more
than Parliament." If the people were to be asked
to fight for their rights, they must at all hazards
not be allowed to say that Congress oppressed them
more than Parliament!

For the moment all this was no more than a
confession that the Association, originally designed as a finely chiseled stepping-stone to reconciliation, was likely to prove a stumbling-block
unless the King graciously extended his royal hand
to give a hearty lift. It presently appeared that
the King refused to extend his hand. October 31,

1775, information reached America that Richard Penn and Arthur Lee, having presented the petition to Lord Dartmouth, were informed that the King would not receive them, and furthermore that no answer would be returned to the Congress. Ignoring the petition was to exhibit only one degree more of contempt for that carefully prepared document than the Congress had shown for Lord North's Resolution on Conciliation; and now that the olive branch had been spurned on both sides, it was a little difficult to see how either side could possibly refuse the sword.

That the colonies would refuse the sword was not very likely; but, as if to make a refusal impossible, the British Government, on December 22, 1775, decided to thrust the sword into their hands. This at all events was thought by many men to be the effect of the Prohibitory Act, which declared the colonies outside the protection of the Crown, and which, for the purpose of reducing them to submission, laid an embargo upon all their trade and proclaimed their ports in a state of blockade.

I know not [John Adams wrote] whether you have seen the Act of Parliament called the Restraining Act or Prohibitory Act, or Piratical Act, or Act of Independency — for by all these titles is it called. I

think the most apposite is the Act of Independency;
the King, Lords, and Commons have united in sunder-
ing this country from that, I think, forever.   It is a
complete dismemberment of the British Empire.   It
throws thirteen colonies out of the royal protection,
and makes us independent in spite of supplications
and entreaties.   It may be fortunate that the act of
Independency should come from the British Parliament rather than from the American Congress; but it
is very odd that Americans should hesitate at accepting such a gift from them.

The majority of those who refused to accept it —
and the number was large — retired, with saddened
hearts for the most part, into the ranks of the British Loyalists; only a few, with John Dickinson at
their head, could still visualize the vanishing image
of reconciliation.   Whether the Prohibitory Act
made reconciliation impossible or not, one thing
at all events it made clear: if Britain was bent on
forcing the colonies to submit by ruining their
trade, it could scarcely be good policy for the colonies to help her do it; of which the reasonable conclusion seemed to be that, since the Parliament
wished to close the ports of America to the world,
Congress would do well to open them to the world.
On February 16, 1776, Congress accordingly took
into "consideration the propriety of opening the

ports." To declare the ports open to the world was
no doubt easily done; but the main thing after all
was to carry on trade with the world; and this was
not so easy since British naval vessels were there
to prevent it. "We can't carry on a beneficial
trade, as our enemies will take our ships"; so Mr.
Sherman said, and of this he thought the obvious
inference was that "a treaty with a foreign power
is necessary, before we open our trade, to protect
it."

"A treaty with a foreign power" — Mr. Wythe
also mentioned this as a possible way of reviving
the trade of the colonies; but a treaty with a
foreign power was easier conceived of than made,
and Mr. Wythe thought "other things are to
be considered before we adopt such a measure."
In considering these "other things," Mr. Wythe
asked and answered the fundamental question:
"In what character shall we treat? — as subjects
of Great Britain — as rebels? . . . If we should
offer our trade to the court of France, would they
take notice of it any more than if Bristol or Liver-
pool should offer theirs, while we profess to be
subjects? No. We must declare ourselves a free
people." Thus it appeared that the character of
British subjects, no less than the Association, was

a stumbling-block in the way of obtaining "the means of carrying on the war." The sword, as an instrument for maintaining rights, could after all not be effectively wielded by America so long as her hand was shackled by even the half-broken ties of a professed allegiance to Britain. Therefore, when the Congress, on the 6th of April, opened the ports of the colonies to the world, the Declaration of Independence was a foregone conclusion.

The idea of independence, for many months past, had hovered like a disembodied hope or menace about the entrance ways of controversy. A few clear-sighted men, such as John Adams and Samuel Seabury, had so long contemplated the idea without blinking that it had taken on familiar form and substance. But the great majority had steadily refused to consider it, except as a possible alternative not needing for the present to be embraced. All these moderate, middle-of-the-way men had now to bring this idea into the focus of attention, for the great illusion that Britain would not push matters to extremities was rapidly dissolving, and the time was come when it was no longer possible for any man to be a British-American and when every man must decide whether it was better to be an American even at the price of rebellion or a Briton even at the price of submission. It is true that many never made up their minds on this point, being quite content to swear allegiance to whichever cause, according to time or place, happened to be in the ascendant. But of all those thinking men whose minds could be made up to stay, perhaps a third — this is the estimate of John Adams — joined the ranks of the British Loyalists; while the rest, with more or less reluctance, gave their support, little or great, to the cause of independence.

When one has made, with whatever reluctance, an irrevocable decision, it is doubtless well to become adjusted to it as rapidly as possible; and this he can best do by thinking of the decision as a wise one — the only one, in fact, which a sensible person could have made. Thus it was that the idea of independence, embraced by most men with reluctance as a last resort and a necessary evil, rapidly lost, in proportion as it seemed necessary, its character of evil, took on the character of the highest wisdom, and so came to be regarded as a predestined event which all honest patriots must rejoice in having had a hand in bringing about.

This change in the point of view would doubtless have been made in any case; but in rapidly investing the idea of independence with the shining virtues of an absolute good to be embraced joyously, a great influence must be ascribed to the little pamphlet entitled *Common Sense*, written by a man then known to good patriots as Thomas Paine, and printed in January, 1776. Intrinsically considered, *Common Sense* was indeed no great performance. The matter, thin at best, was neither profoundly nor subtly reasoned; the manner could hardly be described by even the most complacent critic as humane or engaging. Yet *Common Sense* had its brief hour of fame. Its good fortune was to come at the psychological moment; and being everywhere read during the months from January to July, 1776, it was precisely suited to convince men, not so much that they ought to declare independence, as that they ought to declare it gladly, ought to cast off lightly their former false and mawkish affection for the "mother country" and once for all to make an end of backward yearning looks over the shoulder at this burning Sodom.

To a militant patriot like Thomas Paine it was profoundly humiliating to recall that for ten years past Americans had professed themselves "humble and loyal subjects" and "dutiful children," yielding to none in "admiration" for the "excellent British Constitution," desiring only to live and die as free citizens under the protecting wing of the mother country. Recalling all this sickening sentimentalism, Mr. Paine uttered a loud and ringing Bosh! Let us clear our minds of cant, he said in effect, and ask ourselves what is the nature of government in general and of the famous British Constitution in particular. Like the Abbé Sieyès, Mr. Paine had completely mastered the science of government, which was in fact extremely simple. Men form societies, he said, to satisfy their wants, and then find that governments have to be established to restrain their wickedness; and therefore, since government is obviously a necessary evil, that government is best which is simplest.

Just consider then this "excellent British Constitution," and say whether it is simple. On the contrary, it is the most complicated, irrational, and ridiculous contrivance ever devised as a government of enlightened men. Its admirers say that this complexity is a virtue, on account of the nice balance of powers between King, Lords, and Commons, which guarantees a kind of liberty through the resulting inertia of the whole. The Lords check the Commons and the Commons check the King. But how comes it that the King needs to be checked? Can he not be trusted? This is really the secret of the whole business — that Monarchy naturally tends to despotism; so that the complication of the British Constitution is a virtue only because its basic principle is false and vicious. If Americans still accept the doctrine of the Divine Right of Kings, well and good; if not, then in Heaven's name let them cease to bow down in abject admiration of the British Constitution!

And in ceasing to admire the British Constitution, Americans should also, Thomas Paine thought, give up that other fatal error, the superstition that up to the present unhappy moment the colonies had derived great benefits from living under the protecting wing of the mother country. Protection! "We have boasted the protection of Great Britain, without considering that her motive was interest not attachment; and that she did not protect us from our enemies *on our own account,* but from her enemies *on her own account,* from those who have no quarrel with us *on any other account,* and who will always be our enemies *on the same account.*" An odd sort of protection that, which served only to entangle the colonies in the toils of European intrigues and rivalries, and to make enemies of those who would otherwise be friends! "Our duty to mankind at large, as well as to ourselves, instructs us to renounce the alliance: because, any submission to, or dependence upon, Great Britain, tends directly to involve this continent in European wars and quarrels, and set us at variance with nations who would otherwise seek our friendship and against whom we have neither anger nor complaint."

What foolishness then to seek reconciliation, even if it were possible! Reconciliation at this stage would be the ruin of America. If King George were indeed clever, he would eagerly repeal all the obnoxious acts and make every concession; for when the colonies had once become reconciled he could accomplish by "craft and subtlety, in the long run, what he cannot do by force and violence in the short one." The colonies, having come to maturity, cannot always remain subject to tutelage; like the youth who has reached his majority, they must sooner or later go their own way. Why not now? Beware of reconciliation and of all those who advocate it, for they are either "interested men, who are not to be trusted, weak men who cannot see, prejudiced men who will not see, or a certain set of moderate men who think better of the European world than it deserves."

Such arguments were indeed precisely suited to convince men that independence, so far from being an event in which they had become entangled by the fatal network of circumstance, was an event which they freely willed. "Read by almost every American, and recommended as a work replete with truth, against which none but the partial and prejudiced can form any objection, . . . it satisfied multitudes that it is their true interest immediately to cut the Gordian knot by which the . . . colonists have been bound to Great Britain, and to open their commerce, as an independent people, to all the nations of the world." In April and May, after the Congress had opened the ports, the tide set strongly and irresistibly in the direction of the formal declaration. "Every post and every day rolls in upon us," John Adams said, "Independence like a torrent." It was on the 7th of June that Richard Henry Lee, in behalf of the Virginia delegation and in obedience to the instructions from the Virginia Convention, moved "that these United Colonies are, and of right ought to be, free and independent States . . . ; that it is expedient forthwith to take the most effectual measures for forming foreign Alliances; . . . and that a plan of confederation be prepared and transmitted to the respective Colonies for their consideration and approbation."

The "resolution respecting independency," debated at length, was postponed till the 1st of July, when it was again brought up for consideration. It was still, on that day, opposed by many, chiefly by John Dickinson, who now said that he should not be against independence ultimately, but that he could not consent to it at the present moment because it would serve to divide rather than to unite the colonies.   At the close of the debate on the 1st of July, there seemed little prospect of carrying the resolution by a unanimous vote.   The Delaware deputies were evenly divided, the third member, Cæsar Rodney, not being at the moment in Philadelphia; the Pennsylvania deputies were opposed to the resolution, three against two; while the New York and South Carolina deputies were not in a position to vote at all, having, as they said, no instructions.   The final vote was therefore again postponed until the following day.

Which of the deputies slept this night is not known.   But it is known that Cæsar Rodney, hastily summoned, mounted his horse and rode post-haste to Philadelphia, arriving in time to cast the vote of Delaware in favor of independence; it is known that John Dickinson and Robert Morris remained away from Independence Hall, and that James Wilson changed his mind and voted with Franklin and Morton; and it is known that the South Carolina deputies came somehow to the conclusion, over night, that their instructions were after all sufficient. Thus it was that on July 2, 1776, twelve colonies voted that "these United Colonies are, and of right ought to be, Free and Independent States." One week later, the New York deputies, having been properly instructed, cast the vote of their colony for the resolution also.

Meanwhile, a committee had been appointed to prepare a formal declaration, setting forth the circumstances and the motives which might justify them, in the judgment of mankind, in taking this momentous step. The committee had many meetings to discuss the matter, and, when the main points had been agreed upon, John Adams and Thomas Jefferson were instructed to "draw them up in form, and clothe them in a proper dress." Many years afterwards, in 1822, John Adams related, as accurately as he could.

the conversation which took place when these two met to perform the task assigned them. "Jefferson proposed to me to make the draught. I said, 'I will not.' 'You should do it.' 'Oh! no.' 'Why will you not? You ought to do it.' 'I will not.' 'Why?' 'Reasons enough.' 'What can be your reasons?' 'Reason first — You are a Virginian, and a Virginian ought to appear at the head of this business. Reason second — I am obnoxious, suspected, and unpopular. You are very much otherwise. Reason third — You can write ten times better than I can.' 'Well,' said Jefferson, 'if you are decided, I will do as well as I can.'" In some such manner as this it came about that Thomas Jefferson wrote the Declaration of Independence, no doubt doing, as he said, the best he could.

It is the judgment of posterity that Mr. Jefferson did very well — which was doubtless due partly to the fact that he could write, if not ten times better, at least better than John Adams. Yet the happy phrasing of a brief paragraph or two could scarcely by itself have won so much fame for the author; and perhaps much of the success of this famous paper came from the circumstance that ten years of controversy over the question of political rights had forced Americans to abandon, step by step, the restricted ground of the positive and prescriptive rights of Englishmen and to take their stand on the broader ground of the natural and inherent rights of man. To have said, "We hold this truth to be self-evident: that all Englishmen are endowed by the British Constitution with the customary right of taxing themselves internally" would probably have made no great impression on the sophisticated European mind. It was Thomas Jefferson's good fortune, in voicing the prevailing sentiment in America, to give classic expression to those fundamental principles of a political faith which was destined, in the course of a hundred years, to win the allegiance of the greater part of the western world.

"We hold these truths to be self-evident: that all men are created equal, that they are endowed by their Creator with certain unalienable Rights, that among these, are Life, Liberty, and the pursuit of Happiness. That to secure these rights, Governments are instituted among Men, deriving their just Powers from the consent of the governed. That, whenever any form of Government becomes destructive of these ends, it is the Right of the People to alter or to abolish it, and to institute new Government, laying its foundation on such

Principles and organizing its Powers in such form, as to them shall seem most likely to effect their Safety and Happiness."

It is to these principles — for a generation somewhat obscured, it must be confessed, by the Shining Sword and the Almighty Dollar, by the lengthening shadow of Imperialism and the soporific haze of Historic Rights and the Survival of the Fittest — it is to these principles, these "glittering generalities," that the minds of men are turning again in this day of desolation as a refuge from the cult of efficiency and from faith in "that which is just by the judgment of experience."

BIBLIOGRAPHICAL NOTE

Contemporary Writings: Many of the most important documents for this period are in the following brief collections: W. Macdonald, *Select Charters and Other Documents*, 1906; H. W. Preston, *Documents Illustrative of American History*, 5th ed., 1900; H. Niles, *Principles and Acts of the Revolution in America*, 1822; J. Almon, *Collection of Papers Relative to the Dispute between Great Britain and America*, 1777 (commonly cited as *Prior Documents*). The spirit of the times is best seen in the contemporary newspapers, many extracts from which are printed in F. Moore, *Diary of the American Revolution from the Newspapers and Original Documents*, 1863. Of the numberless controversial pamphlets, the following are noteworthy: J. Otis, *Rights of the British Colonies Asserted and Proved*, 1764; D. Dulaney, *Considerations on the Propriety of Imposing Taxes on the British Colonies*, 1765; J. Dickinson, *Letters from a Farmer in Pennsylvania to the Inhabitants of the British Colonies*, 1768 (also in *Writings of John Dickinson*, 3 vols. 1895); W. Knox, *The Controversy between Great Britain and her Colonies Reviewed*, 1769 (excellent pro-British reply to Dickinson); S. Jenyns, *The Objections to the Taxation of Our American Colonies . . . Briefly Considered*, 1765; J. Wilson, *Considerations on the Nature and Extent of the Legislative Authority of the*

British Parliament, 1774 (also in *The Works of James Wilson,* 2 vols. 1896); S. Seabury, *Free Thoughts on the Proceedings of the Continental Congress,* 1774; T. Paine, *Common Sense,* 1776 (also in *Writings of Thomas Paine,* 4 vols. 1894–96). These pamphlets are not available to most readers, but all of them, together with many others, have been admirably described and summarized in M. C. Tyler, *The Literary History of the American Revolution,* 2 vols. 1897. The letters and public papers of the leaders of the Revolution have been mostly printed, among which some of the most valuable and interesting collections are: C. F. Adams, *The Works of John Adams,* 10 vols. 1856 (vol. II); J. Adams, *Familiar Letters of John Adams and his Wife Abigail Adams,* 1875; W. C. Ford, *The Warren-Adams Letters,* 1917 (vol. I); A. H. Smyth, *The Writings of Benjamin Franklin,* 10 vols. 1905–1907 (vols. IV–VI); P. L. Ford, *The Writings of John Dickinson,* 3 vols. 1895; H. A. Cushing, *The Writings of Samuel Adams,* 4 vols. 1904–1908; P. O. Hutchinson, *Diary and Letters of Thomas Hutchinson,* 2 vols. 1884. The following works give the history of the time as it appeared to various contemporaries: W. Gordon, *History of the Rise, Progress, and Establishment of American Independence,* 4 vols. 1788 (parts of the work taken bodily from the *Annual Register*); D. Ramsey, *History of the Revolution of South Carolina,* 2 vols. 1785; A. Graydon, *Memoirs of His Own Times,* 1846; T. Hutchinson, *History of Massachusetts Bay,* 3 vols. 1795–1828 (based on documents collected by the author, some of which were destroyed in the Stamp Act riots); Mercy Warren, *History of the American Revolution,* 3 vols. 1805 (author was a sister of James Otis); W. Moultrie, *Memoirs of the*

American Revolution so far as it Related to North and South Carolina, 2 vols. 1802; J. Drayton, *Memoirs of the American Revolution*, 2 vols. 1821; T. Jones, *History of New York in the Revolutionary War*, 2 vols. 1879 (by a prominent New York Loyalist); The *Annual Register*, 1765–1776 (an English annual giving summaries of political events supposed to have been prepared by Edmund Burke); H. Walpole, *Memoirs of the Reign of George the Third*, 4 vols. 1894.

Secondary Works: The best single volume on the Revolution is W. E. H. Lecky, *The American Revolution*, 1912. Other good accounts: E. Channing, *History of the United States*, vol. III, 1912; G. Howard, *Preliminaries of the American Revolution*, 1905; S. G. Fisher, *Struggle for American Independence*, 2 vols. 1908 (controverts many traditional ideas. Interesting book by a man who has been bored by the laudation of the heroic and patriotic side of the Revolution). Of the more detailed histories, the best are: G. Bancroft, *History of the United States*, 10 vols. 1834–1874 (vols. V–VIII deal with the period 1765–1776. Strongly prejudiced but accurate as to facts; based on documents collected in European archives, some of which are not easily obtainable elsewhere. Revised ed., 6 vols. 1885, omits notes and references, and therefore not so valuable as the original edition); G. O. Trevelyan, *The American Revolution*, 6 vols. 1899–1914 (brilliantly written by an Englishman of Liberal sympathies. On the whole the work on the Revolution best worth reading). Studies of the beginnings of the Revolution in particular colonies: C. H. Lincoln, *Revolutionary Movement in Pennsylvania*, 1901; H. J. Eckenrode, *The Revolution in Virginia*, 1916; C. L. Becker, *History of Political Parties in New York, 1760–1776,* 1909.   The best account of the British policy leading up to the Grenville measures is G. L. Beer, *British Colonial Policy, 1754–1765,* 1907.   The interesting and important subject of the Loyalists is sketched in C. H. Van Tyne, *The Loyalists of the American Revolution,* 1902.   Interesting biographies well worth reading: W. W. Henry, *Patrick Henry: Life, Correspondence, and Speeches,* 3 vols. 1891; J. K. Hosmer, *Life of Thomas Hutchinson,* 1896; J. K. Hosmer, *Samuel Adams,* 1893; M. Chamberlin, *John Adams,* 1884; C. J. Stillé, *The Life and Times of John Dickinson,* 1891; D. D. Wallace, *Life of Henry Laurens,* 1915; P. L. Ford, *The Many-Sided Franklin,* 1899; J. Parton, *Life and Times of Benjamin Franklin,* 2 vols. 1867.

INDEX

Adams, John, on Virginia Resolutions, 77; attitude on Stamp Act question, 90, 91; defends soldiers, 129; incurs popular displeasure, 129, 152; retires from public affairs, 152; part in Mass. controversy, 185; journeys to first Continental Congress, 200, 208–12; at first Continental Congress, 203, 212–13, 233–34, 235, 236–37; on Prohibitory Act, 242–43; idea of independence, 245; to draft Declaration of Independence with Jefferson, 253; urges Jefferson to write Declaration, 254

Adams, Samuel, Sugar Act protest, 63; abhorrence of Boston riots, 85; attitude on Stamp Act question, 91; assembles town meeting, 128; drafts circular letter, 134–36; on Hutchinson, 150; Otis suspicious of, 152; life and character, 153–58, 160–63; portrait by Copley, 159; leader in crisis, 163–65, 175; controversy with Hutchinson, 176 *et seq.*; goes to first Continental Congress, 200

Adams, Samuel, the elder, 154

Alsop, John, 211, 232

Amherst, Jeffrey, General, 36

Annual Register, 150

Army, Continental, Congress decides to raise, 235

Association of 1774, 219–20, 225–26, 241

Barré, Isaac, Colonel, quoted, 47, 82

Beckford, Alderman, quoted, 41

Bedford, Duke of, 121

Bedford, Grosvenor, Collector of Customs at port of Philadelphia, 13–17

Bernard, Francis, Governor of Mass., corruption, 20; desires changes in colonial government, 21, 22; and finance, 62; and Virginia Resolutions, 76; unable to protect Customs Commissioners, 126; succeeded by Hutchinson, 152; letters to England, 191, 192

Bernard, Nat, Captain of the *Liberty*, 124

Billeting Act, *see* Mutiny Act

Blainville, *see* Céloron de Blainville

Bland, Richard, 66, 71, 74

Boston, Stamp Act riots, 83–86; Customs Commissioners at, 124; *Liberty* sloop riot, 124–26; regiments arrive in (1768), 126–27; Massacre (1770), 127–128; town meeting demands removal of troops, 128; merchants enter non-importation agreement, 139; Hutchinson's account of government, 173–174; town meeting, 174–75; tea party, 199, 206; Port Bill 207, 222

Boston Gazette, 81, 182

Brattle, James. 233